P9-EDL-456

DATE DUE

Atlantis

New and future titles in the series include:

Alien Abductions

Angels

Atlantis

The Bermuda Triangle

The Curse of King Tut

Dragons

Dreams

ESP

The Extinction of the Dinosaurs

Extraterrestrial Life

Fairies

Fortune-Telling

Ghosts

Haunted Houses

The Kennedy Assassination

King Arthur

The Loch Ness Monster

Pyramids

Stonehenge

UFOs

Unicorns

Vampires

Witches

The Mystery Library

Atlantis

Don Nardo

LUCENT
BOOKS®

THOMSON
———✦———
GALE

San Diego • Detroit • New York • San Francisco • Cleveland • New Haven, Conn. • Waterville, Maine • London • Munich

On cover: An idealistic depiction of the Atlantean Mystery Temple by Manly P. Hall (1923).

© 2004 by Lucent Books. Lucent Books is an imprint of The Gale Group, Inc.,
a division of Thomson Learning, Inc.

Lucent Books® and Thomson Learning™ are trademarks used herein under license.

For more information, contact
Lucent Books
27500 Drake Rd.
Farmington Hills, MI 48331-3535
Or you can visit our Internet site at http://www.gale.com

LIBRARY OF CONGRESS CATALOGING-IN-PUBLICATION DATA

Nardo, Don. 1947–
    Atlantis / by Don Nardo.
        p. cm. — (The mystery library)
Summary: Discusses the mystery and theories surrounding Atlantis, a legendary lost continent which Plato wrote about in 399 B.C.
Includes bibliographical references and index.
    ISBN 1-59018-287-1 (hardback : alk. paper)
1. Atlantis—Juvenile literature. [1. Atlantis.] I. Title. II. Mystery library (Lucent books)
    GN751.N37 2004
    001.94—dc22
                                                    2003013854

Printed in the United States of America

Contents

Foreword

In Shakespeare's immortal play *Hamlet*, the young Danish aristocrat Horatio has clearly been astonished and disconcerted by his encounter with a ghostlike apparition on the castle battlements. "There are more things in heaven and earth," his friend Hamlet assures him, "than are dreamt of in your philosophy."

Many people today would readily agree with Hamlet, that the world and the vast universe surrounding it are teeming with wonders and oddities that remain largely outside the realm of present human knowledge or understanding. How did the universe begin? What caused the dinosaurs to become extinct? Was the lost continent of Atlantis a real place or merely legendary? Does a monstrous creature lurk beneath the surface of Scotland's Loch Ness? These are only a few of the intriguing questions that remain unanswered, despite the many great strides made by science in recent centuries.

Lucent Books' Mystery Library series is dedicated to exploring these and other perplexing, sometimes bizarre, and often disturbing or frightening wonders. Each volume in the series presents the best-known tales, incidents, and evidence surrounding the topic in question. Also included are the opinions and theories of scientists and other experts who have attempted to unravel and solve the ongoing mystery. And supplementing this information is a fulsome list of sources for further reading, providing the reader with the means to pursue the topic further.

The Mystery Library will satisfy every young reader's fascination for the unexplained. As one of history's greatest scientists, physicist Albert Einstein, put it:

> The most beautiful thing we can experience is the mysterious. It is the source of all true art and science. He to whom this emotion is a stranger, who can no longer wonder and stand rapt in awe, is as good as dead: his eyes are closed.

Longing for a Land of Beauty and Plenty

In 1870, the renowned French writer Jules Verne, called by many the father of modern science fiction, published *Twenty Thousand Leagues Under the Sea*, about the adventures of the fabulous and futuristic submarine *Nautilus*. At one point in the story, the vessel's master, the brooding Captain Nemo, invites his scientist guest, Professor Pierre Aronnax, to go for a walk on the bottom of the Atlantic Ocean. For a long time, the two men trudge through an underwater world in their cumbersome diving suits. They make their way through what appears to be the remains of an ancient forest and finally they reach the top of a hill. "There, right beneath my eyes," Aronnax later recalls with a touch of excitement,

> lay a town that had been destroyed, completely ruined. Its roofs were open to the sky, its temples fallen, its arches broken, its columns strewn about the ground. . . . Farther off I saw the remains of a gigantic aqueduct—here the high base of an Acropolis, with the floating outline of a Parthenon—yonder the

traces of a quay, as if an ancient port had formerly abutted on the border of the ocean, only one day to disappear forever with its merchant vessels and its war galleys. Such was the sight that Captain Nemo brought before my gaze. Where was I? . . . He picked up from the ground at his feet a piece of chalky stone, walked over to a great rock of black basalt, and traced there one word: ATLANTIS.[1]

Jules Verne did not invent Atlantis, of course. In fact, the story of this supposedly once-great continent in the Atlantic Ocean first appeared some twenty-two centuries before Verne was born. The famous Greek thinker Plato, a native of Athens, introduced Atlantis in two of his philosophical dialogues in the fourth century B.C. According to this account, Atlantis was a powerful and splendid island nation. Long before his own day, Plato wrote, a terrible disaster had occurred and that huge island had sunk beneath the waves.

Greek philosopher Plato wrote of the existence of Atlantis in the fourth century B.C. His descriptions of the lost continent have inspired writers to this day.

A Legend with a Life of Its Own

Plato's description of Atlantis captured the imagination of later ages. The legend of the sunken continent became a favorite subject of poets and other writers, many of whom embellished the tale to suit their own fancies. And the name Atlantis became a symbol of mystery, compelling people in each new generation to wonder about the marvelous achievements of a lost civilization. Indeed, as the centuries rolled by, Atlantis seemed to acquire a life of its own. In the words of Richard Ellis, author of an important, recent book about the lost continent:

> The myth of Atlantis has come down through history as one of the most enduring of all ancient stories. Not a part of any religious cosmography [overview of the world and its place in the universe], the story has lasted for thousands of years without benefit of a proselytizing [missionary] clergy. Where Judeo-Christianity has the Bible, [and] Islam the Koran . . . there is no "religion" based on Atlantean principles, or any sort of a book that might be said to have handed down the wisdom of the ages. . . . It is a story so powerful that it has lasted solely on the basis of its own merits, passed along, often by word of mouth, for two and a half millennia, and today, in an era characterized by technological marvels like atomic energy and the Internet, the legend of Atlantis still thrives.[2]

This mural depicts a busy seaport on a Greek island in the thirteenth century B.C. Some believe the legend of Atlantis comes from an ancient maritime culture.

"Thrives" is perhaps putting it mildly. More than two thousand books and countless articles and short stories have explored the Atlantis mystery. Numerous writers have concocted theories placing the lost continent in nearly every corner of the globe. In the twentieth century alone, proposed sites for Atlantis included not only the Atlantic Ocean, but also South America, North America, the Caribbean islands, the North Sea, Spain, and Antarctica, to name only a few. Some writers have advanced even more fantastic claims—that the Atlanteans possessed technology more advanced than today's, for example, and that the sunken island is scheduled to rise again at any moment.

Almost all of these explorations and explanations of Atlantis take for granted that it was a real place. In the second half of the twentieth century, however, most classical scholars (experts on ancient Greece and Rome) came to the conclusion that Plato was not talking about a real place. Instead, they argue, he based his largely imaginative tale partly on the distorted memory of a maritime people who had inhabited the Greek islands more than a thousand years before his own day. A great deal of convincing evidence has been found to support this thesis; for many scholars, therefore, the mystery of Atlantis has been solved at last.

The Legend Persists

Yet, people in far larger numbers apparently remain unconvinced by this evidence. They still believe, in some cases devoutly, that there was once a continent called Atlantis and that Atlantis was the cradle of human civilization, or at least a powerful empire that controlled or influenced the rest of the world. Plato had access to knowledge now lost about this fabulous place, they insist, and his account must be accepted as factual.

The obvious question is: Why do the mystery and legend of Atlantis persist? One possible answer is that people have always been deeply fascinated by the unknown, the mysterious, and the mythical. Dragons, unicorns, fairies, the Loch Ness monster, Bigfoot, pyramid power, mental telepathy, alien visitations, and the Bermuda Triangle are only some of the better-known concepts in this category. Though all remain unproven, they have consistently captured the popular imagination. Believers point out that some mythical things or places *have* been proven real. The ancient city of Troy, for example, sacked by the Greeks to retrieve the kidnapped beauty Helen, was long thought to be merely fable. Yet, in the late nineteenth century, archaeologists discovered and excavated the city (near Turkey's northwestern coast). If Troy turned out to be real, many would argue, might not Atlantis be proven real, too?

Another reason for the endurance of the Atlantis legend is the understandable human yearning for a better world, or at least a world as admirable as the one that existed in the "good old days." Throughout history, people in many societies have identified with a touch of nostalgia a past time when life was supposedly better. They have "always longed for a land of beauty and plenty," says popular writer L. Sprague de Camp, "where peace and justice reigned. Failing to make one in the real world, they have often sought consolation by creating imaginary Edens, Utopias, and Golden Ages." Indeed, Plato's vision of Atlantis "evokes a picture of a beautiful world with a high and colorful culture (now, alas, gone forever) in the minds of thousands of people who never heard of Plato."[3]

For many people, the suggestion that this "beautiful world" of the past was, in reality, only a distorted memory of a more ordinary ancient society is disappointing. This more mundane Atlantis lacks mystery and glamour. It is neither inspiring nor uplifting nor special, and it forces people to search for the answers to human problems in the present rather than the past. Simply stated, millions of people want to believe that a better place once existed, so the mystery of Atlantis refuses to die. New books about

Atlantis are published each year; some rehash older theories, some propose new ones. This trend is likely to continue for a long time to come. As Camp puts it, the traditional, mysterious, golden, and special Atlantis

> appeals to that hope that most of us carry around in our unconscious, a hope . . . for assurance that somewhere, sometime, there can exist a land of peace and plenty, of beauty and justice. . . . In this sense . . . Atlantis will always be with us.[4]

This modern artist's impression of the lost city of Atlantis shows the beauty and mystery that the name Atlantis evokes for many people.

Chapter 1

Plato's Original Account of Atlantis

Without Plato, there would be no Atlantis. His was the first published account of the fabulous sunken continent, and all later descriptions and interpretations of it either cited or built on what he wrote. The account appears in part, in his *Timaeus,* and in larger part in his *Critias.* These are two of his many dialogues, works in which two or more characters converse on such subjects as politics, history, morality, and justice. Usually, one of the main speakers is Plato's old friend and mentor, Socrates, who was tried and executed by the Athenian state in 399 B.C.

Plato wrote the *Timaeus* and *Critias* about 355 B.C. He was perhaps seventy-two years old at the time and still running the Academy, an institution of higher learning he had established several years before. Originally, he had envisioned writing a trilogy about the events of the distant past. Part one, the *Timaeus,* would deal with the creation of the universe and the Earth; part two, the *Critias*, would describe Atlantis and its ancient war with Athens; and, part three, the *Hermocrates*, would go into more detail about Atlantis and perhaps cover other subjects as well. (The names of these works correspond to the three speakers—Timaeus,

Critias, and Hermocrates—who appear in them along with Socrates. For reasons unknown, however, Plato never finished the *Critias;* indeed, he actually stopped writing in midsentence. He never even began the *Hermocrates.*

In the opening of the *Timaeus,* before the speakers begin discussing the creation, the character Critias briefly mentions the subject that he will deal with in detail in his own dissertation, namely Atlantis. Of what would turn out to be great importance to later generations, he also explains his source of the story of the sunken continent. Critias was Plato's second cousin, and both were descendants of the great Athenian lawgiver Solon, who was born about 630 B.C. Solon had taken a long trip to Egypt, where he had conversed with some local priests; they had told him the story of Atlantis and its ancient war with his own homeland of Athens. Solon then passed on the tale to

The Man Who Introduced Atlantis

Plato was born about 427 B.C. into a well-to-do Athenian family that, through his mother, traced its descent from the renowned Athenian lawgiver Solon. (It was Solon who supposedly heard about the destruction of Atlantis while visiting Egypt.) Little, for certain, is known about Plato's early life except that he grew up during the destructive Peloponnesian War (in its final years he may have served as a cavalryman); and that, through his relatives Critias and Charmides, he became a follower of the eccentric philosopher Socrates. The latter was executed in 399 B.C. on a trumped-up charge of corrupting the city's youth. Devastated, Plato departed Athens and, for the next several years, traveled widely through the Greek world. In 386 B.C. he returned to Athens and established the Academy, a university-like school dedicated to philosophical inquiry. There, he became mentor to the brilliant young Aristotle. Except for a journey to Sicily in the 360s B.C., Plato spent the rest of his life in Athens, running the school and writing, and he died there in 347 B.C. at about the age of eighty. All of his major works have survived to the present. They cover a wide range of topics, but are especially concerned with ethical, moral, political, and legal issues. Most, including the *Timaeus* and *Critias,* which contain his account of Atlantis, take the form of a dialogue in which two or more characters engage in a session of questions and answers. The central character is usually Socrates, his old mentor.

Critias's great-grandfather, Dropides. In turn, Dropides "told the story to Critias, my grandfather," says the living Critias, "who remembered and repeated it to us."[5]

A Thumbnail Sketch of Atlantis

Having identified the source of his information about Atlantis, Critias goes on in the *Timaeus* to provide a thumbnail sketch of the lost island. "Many great and wonderful deeds are recorded of your state [i.e., Athens] in our histories," the Egyptian priests supposedly told Solon:

The Rock of Gibraltar guards the strait connecting the Mediterranean Sea with the Atlantic Ocean. The ancients knew the strait as the Pillars of Heracles.

> But one of them exceeds all the rest in greatness and valor. For these histories tell of a mighty power which unprovoked made an expedition against the whole of Europe and Asia, and to which your city put an end. This power came forth out of the Atlantic Ocean, for in those days the Atlantic was navigable; and there was an island situated in front of the straits which are by you called the Pillars of Heracles.[6]

In Plato's day, the Pillars of Heracles (whom the Romans called Hercules) was the common Greek name for the Strait of Gibraltar, the narrow waterway connecting the Mediterranean Sea and Atlantic Ocean. This has led many people to assume that Atlantis existed in the Atlantic Ocean. (People also assume that one was named after the other; however, the two names may well have very different derivations.)

Next, Critias addresses Atlantis's size. "The island was larger than Libya and Asia put together," he says. This statement can be deceiving from a modern viewpoint. In the fourth century B.C., the Greeks had no realistic conception of the actual size of Asia. In using the term, therefore, Plato likely meant what today is called the Middle East, which, combined with Libya (part of North Africa), is still a very large area. Atlantis was also "the way to other islands," Critias adds,

> and from these you might pass to the whole of the opposite continent which surrounded the true ocean; for this sea which is within the Straits of Heracles [i.e., the Mediterranean] is only a harbor, having a narrow entrance, but that other [the Atlantic] is a real sea, and the surrounding land may be most truly called a boundless continent.[7]

Having identified Atlantis and emphasized its huge size, Critias describes it as the center of a powerful empire that included nearby islands and parts of Europe. Atlantis, says Critias, subjugated much of western Europe (presumably including what is now Britain, France, and Spain) and large parts of North Africa. Then the Atlanteans launched an aggressive war against Egypt and Greece. Fortunately for the Egyptians and Greeks, however, Athens rose to the occasion. "Then, Solon," the Egyptian priests asserted (according to Critias), your country shone forth, in the excellence of her virtue and strength, among all mankind. She was pre-eminent in courage and military skill, and was the leader of the Hellenes [Greeks]. And when the rest [of the Greek states] fell off from [abandoned] her, being compelled to stand alone, after having undergone the very extremity of danger, she defeated and triumphed over the invaders, and preserved from slavery those who were not yet subjugated, and generously liberated all the rest of us who dwell within the pillars.[8]

Critias's brief, initial sketch of Atlantis ends with an equally brief description of the island's sudden destruction:

But afterwards there occurred violent earthquakes and floods; and in a single day and night of misfortune all your warlike men in a body sank into the earth, and the island of Atlantis in like manner disappeared in the depths of the sea. For which reason the sea in those parts is impassable and impenetrable, because there is a shoal of mud in the way; and this was caused by the subsidence of the island.[9]

Creation of the Central Metropolis

In the *Critias*, Plato's character Critias goes into considerably more detail about Atlantis, its land, its cities, and its people, than he did in the *Timaeus*. First he tells his listeners that nine thousand years have elapsed since the great war he described earlier. Then he devotes considerable space to the manner in which the societies of both Atlantis and Athens developed in the years preceding the war. The gods divided up the various parts of the world among themselves, he says. Athena, goddess of wisdom and war, and Hephaestos, god of the forge, took charge of Athens, while Poseidon, ruler of the seas, became the master of Atlantis. These divinities made sure their lands were well stocked with humans and animals. They also taught the people how to support and govern themselves.

The mighty Poseidon saw that a mountain with a gentle slope on all sides rested in the center of the island of Atlantis. Around this mountain he constructed concentric rings of water and land, each ring nesting within another. In a way, the watery rings were like huge, circular harbors and the earthen rings like circular islands. He also stretched forth his trident (three-pronged spear), one of his symbols,

The figure of Poseidon, the trident-wielding Greek god of the sea, adorns this fifth-century B.C. vase. Poseidon was the legendary ruler of Atlantis.

and caused two springs to rise up from the ground. One flowed with cold water, the other with warm water. Then Poseidon fathered ten male children born to a local woman named Cleito, divided the island into ten sections, and made each of the boys ruler of one section.

In time, the descendants of these rulers built a magnificent civilization on Atlantis, which was blessed with abundant animal life, forests, and fertile soil. Critias tells how they constructed harbors, docks, and a splendid palace in the island's central metropolis (city):

> They arranged the whole country in the following manner. First of all they bridged over the [circular] zones of sea [created earlier by Poseidon], which surrounded the ancient metropolis, making a road to and from the royal palace. And at the very beginning they built the palace in the habitation of the god and of their ancestors, which they continued to ornament in successive generations, every king surpassing the one who went before him to the utmost of his power, until they made the building a marvel to behold for size and for beauty. And beginning from the sea they bored a canal of three hundred feet in width and one hundred feet in depth and fifty stadia [six miles] in length, which they carried through to the outermost zone, making a passage from the sea up to this, which became a harbor, and leaving an opening sufficient to enable the largest vessels to find ingress [entrance]. Moreover, they divided at the bridges the zones of land which parted the zones of sea, leaving room for a single trireme [ship with three banks of oars] to pass out of one zone into another, and they covered over the channels so as to leave a way underneath for the ships; for the banks were raised considerably above the water.[10]

The palace was huge, hundreds of feet in length and width. It was also richly decorated with gold, silver, and orichalcum (a shiny yellow metal) and, Critias says, had "a strange barbaric appearance."[11]

Atlantis's Great Plain and Army

Next, Critias leaves the central city behind and describes the countryside of Atlantis, beginning with its large, flat, continental plain:

> The whole country was said by him to be very lofty and precipitous on the side of the sea, but the country immediately about and surrounding the city was a level plain, itself surrounded by mountains which descended towards the sea; it was smooth and even, and of an oblong shape, extending in one direction three thousand stadia [340 miles], but across the center inland it was two thousand stadia [230

Atlantis's Abundant Animals and Plants

In this excerpt from the *Critias* (translated by Benjamin Jowett), Plato discusses Atlantis's animals and vegetation.

There were a great number of elephants in the island; for as there was provision for all other sorts of animals, both for those which live in lakes and marshes and rivers, and also for those which live in mountains and on plains, so there was for the animal which is the largest and most voracious of all. Also whatever fragrant things there now are in the earth, whether roots, or herbage, or woods, or essences which distill from fruit and flower, grew and thrived in that land; also the fruit which admits of cultivation, both the dry sort . . . and the fruits having a hard rind, affording drinks and meats and ointments, and good store of chestnuts and the like, which furnish pleasure and amusement, and are fruits which spoil with keeping, and the pleasant kinds of dessert, with which we console ourselves after dinner, when we are tired of eating—all these that sacred island which then beheld the light of the sun, brought forth fair and wondrous and in infinite abundance. With such blessings the earth freely furnished them.

miles]. This part of the island looked towards the south, and was sheltered from the north.[12]

In this very fertile plain, which produced every kind of crop imaginable, were numerous rivers and lakes. These supplied abundant water to the many comfortable and prosperous villages that existed in the plain.

According to the story passed down to Critias and Plato by Solon, a certain number of the people who dwelled in these villages were required to serve in the Atlantean army. Details about the army are important, since the story emphasizes Atlantis's conquests in Europe and its war with Athens. For military purposes, Critias explains, the great plain and hill country of Atlantis were divided into sixty thousand lots of land (each lot being a square about six thousand feet on a side). Each lot had a local leader who was responsible for supplying his king with men and weapons. "The leader," Critias asserts,

> was required to furnish for the war the sixth portion of a war-chariot, so as to make up a total of ten thousand chariots; also two horses and riders for them, and a pair of chariot-horses without a seat, accompanied by a horseman who could fight on foot carrying a small shield, and having a charioteer who stood behind the man-at-arms to guide the two horses; also, he was bound to furnish two heavy armed soldiers, two slingers, three stone-shooters and three javelin-men, who were light-armed, and four sailors to make up the complement of twelve hundred ships.[13]

Atlantean Government and Religious Ritual

The ten kings of Atlantis (each in charge of his portion of the island, as Poseidon had ordained years before) were the commanders of the army. In addition, each of these men ruled his own territory as he saw fit, meting out punishment and reward at will. He did have to abide by a higher law of the land, however. Although each king was an absolute monarch, he had to follow a set of laws that had been issued by Poseidon, himself. These laws were inscribed on a pillar of orichalcum that stood in the god's sacred temple in the island's central metropolis.

Near this temple, once every five or six years, the ten rulers met to discuss their common interests. They also had the right to accuse one another of wrongdoing, at which point nine of them could judge a tenth who had transgressed. This political arrangement had obviously been installed by Poseidon to keep any one of the kings from gaining significant power over the others. The laws regarding the arrangement were clear:

> They [the ten kings] were not to take up arms against one another, and they were all to come to the rescue if any one in any of their cities attempted to overthrow the royal house; like their ancestors, they were to deliberate in common about war and other matters. . . . And the king [of any one section of Atlantis] was not to have the power of life and death over any of his kinsmen unless he had the assent of the majority of the ten. Such was the vast power which the god settled in the lost island of Atlantis.[14]

Whenever they met in council, the kings had to swear an oath to uphold these and Poseidon's other laws. The oath was bound up in a complex religious ritual that involved the sacrifice of a bull (which, in such a ceremony, was called the victim). Bulls were apparently central to Atlantean worship. Indeed, according to Critias's account, bulls were sacred animals that were allowed to roam freely in parts of Poseidon's great temple. The solemn religious ceremony in which the kings (and, perhaps, others) took part included capturing a bull in a very specific manner and

The Atlantean Temple of Poseidon

In the *Critias*, Plato gives this description (translated by Benjamin Jowett) of the ornate temple erected in the island's central metropolis.

Here was Poseidon's own temple which was a stadium [some six hundred feet] in length, and half a stadium in width, and of a proportionate height, having a strange barbaric appearance. All the outside of the temple, with the exception of the pinnacles, they covered with silver, and the pinnacles with gold. In the interior of the temple the roof was of ivory, curiously wrought everywhere with gold and silver and orichalcum [a shiny yellow metal]; and all the other parts, the walls and pillars and floor, they coated with orichalcum. In the temple they placed statues of gold. There was the god himself standing in a chariot—the charioteer of six winged horses—and of such a size that he touched the roof of the building with his head. . . . There were also in the interior of the temple other images which had been dedicated by private persons.

And around the temple on the outside were placed statues of gold of all the descendants of the ten kings [of Atlantis] and of their wives, and there were many other great offerings of kings and of private persons, coming both from the city itself and from the foreign cities over which they held sway. There was an altar too, which in size and workmanship corresponded to this magnificence, and the palaces, in like manner, answered to the greatness of the kingdom and the glory of the temple.

This modern illustration of Atlantis depicts the great temple of Poseidon that dominated the lost city's skyline.

then killing and dedicating the animal to the god according to set rules:

A gold goblet from the tomb of a Greek king is adorned with the figures of a bull and a man. Bulls were central to Atlantean religious worship.

There were bulls who had the range of the temple of Poseidon; and the ten kings, being left alone in the temple, after they had offered prayers to the god that they might capture the victim which was acceptable to him, hunted the bulls, without weapons but with staves [wooden sticks] and nooses; and the bull which they caught they led up to the pillar and cut its throat over the top of it so that the blood fell upon the sacred inscription. Now on the pillar, besides the laws, there was inscribed an oath invoking mighty curses on the disobedient. When therefore, after slaying the bull in the accustomed manner, they had burnt its limbs, they filled a bowl of wine and cast in a clot of blood for each of them; the rest of the victim they put in the fire, after having purified the column all round. Then they drew from the bowl in golden cups and . . . swore that they would judge according to the laws on the pillar, and . . . that for the future they would not . . . offend against the writing on the pillar, and would [not] . . . act otherwise than according to the laws of their father Poseidon. This was the prayer which each of them offered up for himself and for his descendants, at the same time drinking and dedicating the cup out of which he drank in the temple of the god.[15]

A Mystery That Would Never Die

Abiding by this sacred oath and prayer, the Atlantean kings long ruled justly and well, Critias says, always upholding Poseidon's laws. Eventually, however, they began to grow corrupt. What happened next, and whether this corruption led to the war with Athens, is unknown. The narrator is in the midst of telling how the chief god, Zeus, had become angry with the Atlanteans over their fall from grace when the *Critias* abruptly ends. Fortunately, the brief summary provided by the character Critias in the *Timaeus* reveals that there was a war, and also that Atlantis was eventually destroyed by earthquakes and floods.

Considering the level of detail Plato supplied about Atlantis in these two works, it is only natural to wonder whether he believed the story was true. Regrettably, there is no way to know. There is also no way to know how much of the story already existed and how much came from Plato's own imagination. But, in the larger scheme of Atlantean literature and studies, it is irrelevant whether he believed the lost continent was real or imaginary or whether he inflated the tale. All he cared about was using the legend to get across the moral of his story. Indeed, judging by everything Plato wrote, he had to have some lesson in mind. "It is extremely unlikely," Richard Ellis writes,

> that one of the world's foremost thinkers would embellish one of his philosophical [inquiries] with a story about a city that was swallowed up by the sea unless it served a purpose, and since Plato was particularly interested in ideal societies—see, for example, the *Republic* [his dialogue describing a society ruled by philosopher-kings]—it does not seem unrealistic or illogical to interpret the story of the disappearance of Atlantis as a parable, a story to illustrate a moral or religious lesson.[16]

Perhaps the lesson was that even the best and mightiest nations can eventually become corrupt and fall. Whatever Plato's moral may have been, though, it proved of little interest to later generations. As his account was read and reread over the centuries, the element that people found most fascinating was the existence of a great island empire that sank into the sea. Even if Plato, himself, viewed Atlantis as fanciful, the vast majority of people in later ages took the story seriously and accepted the lost continent as a real place. The great thinker had no way of knowing that he had initiated both a mystery and a craze that would never die.

Chapter 2

The Modern World Rediscovers Atlantis

In the generations immediately following Plato's death in 347 B.C., scholars across the Mediterranean world became familiar with his story of Atlantis as told in the *Timaeus* and *Critias*. A number of these scholars commented about the story in their own works, and, in turn, passed the tale of Atlantis down to later generations. Eventually the tale reached the early modern world, where new generations of writers began to reexamine it. Large numbers of books appeared on the subject, some of which were widely read in Europe and the United States. This exposure gained Atlantis international recognition, as well as what might be called a cult following, a legion of devotees who were and remain convinced it was a real place. Of their number, those who research and write books about the subject are often referred to as Atlantologists (or Atlantists).

How the Ancients Viewed Atlantis

It is perhaps revealing that the belief that Atlantis was real did not develop until several centuries after Plato's time. In fact, his famous pupil, the philosopher Aristotle, apparently assumed that Plato fabricated the story to make some moral or literary point. Aristotle's actual commentary on the subject is, unfortunately, lost. However, the first-century B.C. Greek geographer Strabo briefly mentions a remark by Aristotle to the effect that Atlantis was a Platonic invention.

Plato's famous pupil Aristotle (pictured) believed his teacher's tale of Atlantis was a fable.

Most of the Greek writers who followed Aristotle were also skeptical of the reality of Plato's tale and examined at least parts of the story with a critical eye. The noted first-century A.D. biographer Plutarch, for example, seemed to think that Atlantis was largely a literary fiction. He accepted the assertion that the Egyptian priests had told Solon about a legendary island that had sunk into the sea; however, Plutarch pointed out, Solon thought the story was good material for an epic poem:

> Solon also attempted to write a long poem dealing with the story or legend of the lost Atlantis, because the subject, according to what he had heard from the learned [Egyptian priests], had a special connection with Athens. He finally abandoned it, however, not, as Plato suggests, for lack of time, but rather because of his age and his fear that the task would be too much for him.[17]

Plutarch's Mysterious Island

In his essay "The Face of the Moon," in his *Moralia*, the first-century Greek writer Plutarch presents an imaginary dialogue between two men. One, a Carthaginian named Sulla, tells about a mysterious island he had once visited in the great ocean lying west of Europe. He also makes reference to another fabulous isle in those largely unknown waters—Ogygia, which first appeared in the Greek poet Homer's famous epic the *Odyssey*. It is clear that this tract was influenced by Plato's tale of Atlantis, written some four centuries earlier.

[The island is] a run of five days off from Britain as you sail westward; and three other islands equally distant from it and from one another lie out from it in the general direction of the summer sunset. In one of these, according to the tale told by the natives, [the ancient god] Cronos is confined by Zeus. . . . The great mainland [world continent?] by which the great ocean is encircled, while not so far from the other islands, is about five thousand stades [600 miles] from Ogygia, the voyage being made by oar, for the main is slow to traverse and muddy as a result of the multitude of streams.

Later, Plutarch says, the task of embellishing the legend for literary purposes fell to Solon's descendant Plato:

> Plato was particularly ambitious to create an elaborate masterpiece out of the subject of Atlantis, as if it were a site on some fine estate, which was still unbuilt on, but to which he had a special claim by virtue of his connection with Solon, and he began the task by laying out great porches and enclosures and courtyards [supposedly in Atlantis] on a magnificent scale, such as no story or myth or poetic creation had ever received before. But he was late in beginning [i.e., he was an old man when he began writing] and the task proved too long for his lifetime. . . . Among the many beautiful works which Plato's vision conceived, the tale of the lost Atlantis is the only one to be left unfinished.[18]

As time went on, however, classical writers became increasingly less critical of the Atlantis story. This was especially true of Roman and Romanized Greek writers. In the fourth century, for instance, Ammianus Marcellinus, the greatest Roman historian of the later Roman Empire, matter-of-factly reported the sinking of a large island in the Atlantic long before his time. A century later the Greek philosopher Proclus, who wrote commentaries on Plato's works, completely accepted the reality of Atlantis. "That such and so great an island once existed," he stated,

> is evident by what is said by certain historians respecting what pertains to the external sea. For according to them, there were seven islands in that sea . . . and also three others of immense extent, one of which was sacred to . . . Poseidon. . . . They also add that the inhabitants of it [the island] preserved the remembrance of their ancestors, or the Atlantic island that existed there . . . which for many periods

had domination over all the islands in the Atlantic. . . . It is not proper to disbelieve what is said by Plato. . . . It should be received as a mere history.[19]

Atlantis in the Americas?

This tendency to take the Atlantis story at face value fore-shadowed the equally uncritical approach many modern writers have taken to the subject. Well before those writers picked up their pens, however, the lost continent was, in a sense, lost once more. Flourishing shortly before Rome's fall, Proclus was one of the last ancient literary figures to mention Atlantis. And medieval writers showed little interest in the lost continent. L. Sprague de Camp explains why:

> The rise of Christianity and the decline of the Roman Empire shifted intellectual interest from the things of this world to those of the next. Interest in remote events of mundane history, including Atlantis, declined. . . . Atlantis would seem to have sunk a second time, since, save for a brief mention in [a] medieval encyclopedia . . . nothing more [was] heard of it for many centuries. Still, the cult was not dead, merely dormant.[20]

Indeed, Atlantis was destined to rise again. The first major stimulus to its revival was Europe's discovery and early exploration of the Americas. In 1553, a Spanish historian named Francesco Lopez de Gomara proposed a novel idea that seemed very logical at the time. He insisted that the Atlantic continent mentioned by Plato was none other than the landmass of North America and South America. In this view, Plato had been wrong about the continent's sinking but right about its existence. Some people who accepted this idea pointed to what they saw as proof. The Aztecs, natives of what is now Mexico, had a legend that their ancestors came from a place called Aztlan, a name

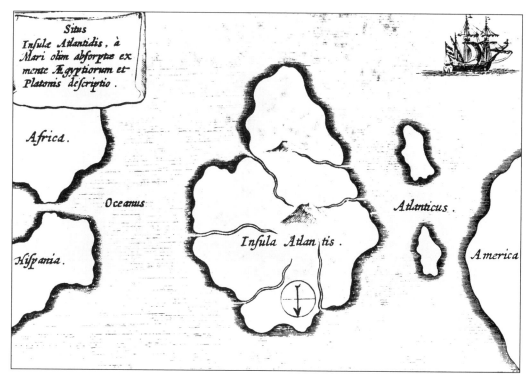

This seventeenth-century Dutch map positions Atlantis midway between America and southern Europe.

somewhat similar to Atlantis. Gomara's theory remained popular in the seventeenth century, thanks in part to its promotion by English writers Francis Bacon and John Swan. Swan suggested that Atlantis was North America, part of which sank a few thousand years before Plato's time, giving rise to the legend.

The theory that Atlantis was America eventually fell out of favor, however, mainly because it was not able to explain other claims put forth in Plato's account. It became clear that the Native Americans had not possessed a sophisticated civilization in the dim past, for example. Nor had they ever had the naval capacity to send expeditions across the Atlantic Ocean to Europe.

Enter Ignatius Donnelly

Therefore, later writers returned to the older idea that Atlantis was situated in the Atlantic Ocean, a lost continent

Nineteenth-century American writer Ignatius Donnelly wrote the most influential book on Atlantis of modern times.

that had once floated halfway between Europe and the Americas. That meant that Atlantis could have had just as much contact with the Americas as it had with Europe. A few people went so far as to suggest that the Atlanteans had been the first civilized humans and that they had carried civilized customs and ideas to other parts of the globe.

This tantalizing idea became the main thesis of the most widely read and influential book about Atlantis written in modern times—*Atlantis: The Antediluvian World*, first published in 1882. (Antediluvian means "before the great flood," or extremely ancient.) The author was Ignatius Donnelly, one of the most ambitious, if least skilled, scholars of his century. He was born in Philadelphia and later moved to Minnesota, where he ran a small newspaper and eventually won election to Congress. After eight years as a legislator, he returned to Minnesota and wrote his massive tome about Atlantis. The following statement from the book sums up his belief that the lost continent was the very fountainhead (original source) of civilization:

> Surely there is no study which appeals more strongly to the imagination than that of this drowned nation, the true antediluvians. They were the founders of nearly all our arts and sciences; they were the parents of our fundamental beliefs; they were the first civilizers, the first navigators, the first merchants, the first colonizers of the earth; their civilization

was old when Egypt was young, and they had passed away thousands of years before Babylon, Rome, or London were dreamed of. This lost people were our ancestors, their blood flows in our veins; the words we use every day were heard, in their primitive form, in their cities, courts, and temples. Every line of race and thought, of blood and belief, leads back to them.[21]

Donnelly's book begins with his now famous thirteen propositions, which became almost holy writ to his many followers and have permeated the literature about Atlantis ever since. First, he said, Atlantis was a large island situated in the Atlantic Ocean. Second, Plato's account of Atlantis was not fiction but historical fact, and third, humans first rose from barbarism in Atlantis. Fourth, people from Atlantis eventually migrated to North and South America, Europe, Africa, and elsewhere. The fifth proposition states that Atlantis was the Garden of Eden, as well as the Greek Mount Olympus (where the Greek gods supposedly dwelled), and represented "a universal memory of a great land, where early mankind dwelt for ages in peace and happiness."[22] Sixth, the gods and goddesses of the Greeks and other ancient peoples were the kings, queens, and heroes of Atlantis. Seventh, the original religion of Atlantis was sun worship, which survived in Egypt and Peru. And eighth, the oldest Atlantean colony was in Egypt.

The remaining propositions are:

9. That the implements of the "Bronze Age" of Europe were derived from Atlantis. The Atlanteans were also the first manufacturers of iron.

10. That the Phoenician alphabet, parent of all European alphabets, was derived from an Atlantis alphabet, which was also conveyed from Atlantis to the Mayas of Central America.

11. That Atlantis was the original seat of the Aryan or Indo-European family of nations, as well as of Semitic peoples.

12. That Atlantis perished in a terrible convulsion of nature, in which the whole island was submerged by the ocean, with nearly all its inhabitants.

Did the Atlanteans Invent the Pyramid?

Here, from his widely read 1882 book about Atlantis, Ignatius Donnelly, sometimes referred to as the father of Atlantology, gives an example of what he sees as the diffusion of Atlantean culture to both sides of the Atlantic. (Note that he mainly asks the reader to draw the same conclusions he has drawn but provides no concrete evidence to prove them.)

Were not the pyramids of Egypt and America imitations of similar structures in Atlantis? Might not the building of such a gigantic edifice have given rise to the legends existing on both continents in regard to the Tower of Babel? How did the human mind hit upon this singular edifice—the pyramid? By what process of development did it reach it? Why should these extraordinary structures crop out on the banks of the Nile, and amid the forests and plains of America? And why, in both countries,

should they stand with their sides square to the four cardinal points of the compass? Are they in this, too, a reminiscence of the Cross, and of the four rivers of Atlantis that ran to the north, south, east, and west? . . . We find the pyramid on both sides of the Atlantic, with its four sides pointing, like the arms of the Cross, to the four cardinal points—a reminiscence of Olympus; and in the Aztec representation of Olympus (Aztlan) we find the pyramid as the central and typical figure. Is it possible to suppose all these extraordinary coincidences to be the result of accident?

Donnelly believed the design of the great pyramids of Egypt came from Atlantis.

13. That a few persons escaped in ships and on rafts, and carried to the nations east and west the tidings of the appalling catastrophe, which has survived to our own time in Flood and Deluge legends in the different nations of the Old and New Worlds.[23]

Lacking in Critical Judgment

Of these bold statements, numbers 4 through 11 propose that various key elements of the centralized Atlantean civilization filtered outward in all directions, implanting political, social, religious, and artistic seeds that soon grew into the known civilizations of the ancient world. This is an example of what scholars call cultural diffusion—the spread of cultural ideas from one place to another, as opposed to these ideas growing up independently in different places. As noted scholar Rodney Castleden explains:

> Donnelly's arguments depended on the diffusionist theory of culture. If pyramids were found in Egypt and Latin America and the decimal system of counting was found among Peruvians and Anglo-Saxons, people must have traveled from one area to another, taking the concepts and techniques needed for pyramid-building and decimal counting with them. Placing a landmass in the Atlantic Ocean would make this diffusion easier by shortening the sea journeys involved. Once the heartland sank under the waves, the colonies developed separately, but still displaying vestiges of the original culture.[24]

Donnelly's book certainly presents a mountain of comparisons of and correlations between Old and New World cultures. Indeed, the enormous amount of detailed information he cites is enough to bewilder, impress, and win over the average nonscholar. The problem is that Donnelly seriously lacked critical judgment. Page after page of the work is riddled with misleading generalizations, circular reasoning, and/or unwarranted conclusions. "Since Donnelly's formidable learning is likely to stun the average reader into taking his statements at face value," Camp writes,

Despite the scholarly shortcomings of Donnelly's book on Atlantis, his work inspired new generations of Atlantologists.

a close look at his book is needed to show how careless, tendentious [biased], and generally worthless it is. For instance, to point out that both Europeans and Amerinds [early inhabitants of the Americas] used spears and sails; that both practiced marriage and divorce; and that both believed in ghosts and flood-legends, proves nothing about sunken continents, but only that the peoples in question were all human beings, since all these customs and beliefs are practically world-wide. Most of Donnelly's statements of fact . . . either were wrong when he made them, or have been disproved by subsequent discoveries. It is not true, as he stated, that the Peruvian Indians had a system of writing, that the cotton-plants native to the New and Old Worlds belong to the same species, [or] that Egyptian civilization sprang suddenly into being.[25]

IGNATIUS DONNELLY

ATLAN-TIS

THE ANTEDILUVIAN WORLD

A MODERN REVISED EDITION

EDITED BY

EGERTON SYKES

Credible and Less than Credible Claims

The fact that Donnelly was a sloppy scholar does not mean that his basic thesis about Atlantis was wrong or that it had any less impact. Regardless of the shortcomings of the book, it profoundly influenced new generations of Atlantologists who insisted that Atlantis was a large island in the Atlantic Ocean. A few of these individuals were legitimate scholars who were considerably more careful and critical than Donnelly.

The most prominent and influential of their number was a Scottish anthropologist named Lewis Spence. He published *The Problem of Atlantis* in 1924 and followed that with four more volumes on the subject. Spence suggested that there had been two large islands in the Atlantic— Atlantis, located near Europe, and Antillia, in the Caribbean region. Atlantis sank, he said, about 10,000 B.C., roughly in the period attested by Plato. (In contrast, Antillia sank more recently, and only partially, leaving behind the many Caribbean islands.)

However, Spence rejected large portions of Plato's narrative, saying, for example, that the war between Atlantis and Athens was likely fictional or a distorted memory of some later Greek conflict. Spence declared that Plato was also wrong about the Atlanteans' having metals. Instead, Spence proposed, Atlantis had a Stone Age culture. In his view, the Atlanteans were the Cro-Magnon people, who used stone tools and whose drawings of animals have been found on the walls of caves in France. Thus, the European Cro-Magnons originally came from the west—from Atlantis.

In the years since Spence wrote his books, new evidence has shown that many of his ideas were questionable and some were just plain wrong. For instance, it is now known that the Cro-Magnons entered Europe from the east, not from the west. Still, Spence's attempt to verify the lost continent's existence was at least honest and credible. Many others involved in the modern rediscovery of Plato's Atlantis were less than honest or much less credible. In 1912, for example, Paul Schliemann, grandson of the renowned archaeologist Heinrich Schliemann (who excavated Troy), claimed to possess some coins and other artifacts belonging to a king of Atlantis. That turned out to be a lie, but for decades afterward the younger Schliemann was seen by many as an authority on Atlantis.

Perhaps even more damaging to the reputation of honest research in Atlantology were the claims of self-styled mystics, psychics, and other dabblers in the occult. The most famous was Edgar Cayce, a native of Kentucky who died in 1945. Cayce purported to go into trances, during which he gave "readings," streams of information that included diagnoses of people's illnesses. He also claimed to be able to see into the past and future. According to Cayce, many people of his day were reincarnated Atlanteans, and through them he learned that Atlantis had advanced technology, including electricity, airplanes, and an energy source similar to nuclear power.

Cayce never provided any tangible proof for his wild claims. Further damaging his credibility was the fact that most of his major prophecies did not come true. For instance, he predicted that between 1958 and 1998 Los Angeles and New York would be destroyed and most of Japan would sink into the sea. He also said that Atlantis would begin to rise from the floor of the Atlantic in 1968. None of these momentous events happened, of course. And, since Cayce's ability to see into the future was poor at best, one cannot help but question the accuracy of his visions of the past, including his claims about Atlantis.

One thing that Plato, Donnelly, Spence, and Cayce all had in common was their belief that Atlantis was located in

The Atlantean Artifact Hoax

In this excerpt from his informative book *Lost Continents*, scholar L. Sprague de Camp tells about the Atlantis-related hoax perpetrated by Paul Schliemann in 1912.

Schliemann said that his grandfather [the great archaeologist Heinrich Schliemann] had left him a batch of papers on archeological matters and an owl-headed vase of ancient provenance. The envelope containing the papers bore a warning that the envelope should only be opened by a member of Schliemann's family willing to swear to devote his life to research into the matters dealt with in the papers inside. Paul Schliemann took the pledge and opened the envelope. The first instruction was to break open the vase. Inside he found some square coins of platinum-aluminum-silver alloy, and a metal plate inscribed in Phoenician: "Issued in the Temple of Transparent Walls." Among his grandfather's notes he came across an account of finding a large bronze vase on the site of Troy, in which were coins and other artifacts of metal, bone, and pottery. The vase and some of the subjects were inscribed: "From King Cronos of Atlantis." . . . Schliemann promised to reveal the full story of his discoveries in a book . . . [saying,] "But if I desired to say everything I know, there would be no more mystery about it." Alas, the book never appeared; nor were there any further revelations. . . . The evident fact that the whole thing was a hoax has not stopped Atlantists from quoting the younger Schliemann as an authority, sometimes confusing him with his grandfather.

the Atlantic Ocean. But the modern rediscovery of the lost continent also led to a new way of viewing the Atlantis story. Many writers suspected that Plato might have been mistaken when he said that Atlantis was in the Atlantic and they began searching for it in other parts of the world. As these proposed locales multiplied, the mystery of the sunken continent grew deeper, more complex, and more fascinating.

Chapter 3

Searching for Atlantis Around the Globe

Stating that Atlantis might possibly have existed is one thing; providing proof of its location is quite another. Indeed, finding definitive proof to back up their claims has always been a stumbling block for advocates of a historical Atlantis. When Ignatius Donnelly established the modern cult of Atlantis more than a century ago, he did so using circumstantial evidence, most of which could be interpreted in other ways or was simply misguided. Yet, he inspired numerous popular writers, psychics, and even a few scientists to launch their own searches for the lost continent. And most of them at least tried to give convincing evidence to back up their claims.

Some of these searchers attempted, as Donnelly had, to show that Atlantis was located in the Atlantic Ocean. But others felt that perhaps Donnelly and his supporters had taken Plato's account too literally. In this view, a lot of history had transpired in the nine thousand years separating

Atlantis's demise from Plato's writings. In all those centuries, entire peoples, nations, cultures, and languages must have disappeared or undergone much change, and a great deal of information about the real Atlantis was likely either forgotten or transformed into distorted memories, often in the form of myths. It made sense, therefore, that the story given to Solon by the Egyptian priests was itself a distorted memory of real places and events. In that case, the priests, Solon, and Plato may have mistakenly placed Atlantis in the Atlantic Ocean when it was really somewhere else.

Based on this logic, as well as other factors, over the years Atlantologists proposed a surprisingly large number of alternative locations for the mysterious Atlantean island. Among these were Morocco, Tunisia, and various other locations in Africa. European locales, such as central France, the Netherlands, Portugal, the island of Malta (in

Atlantis in the Caribbean?

One consistently popular location for Atlantis is in the Caribbean region. Here, from *Gateway to Atlantis*, Andrew Collins makes his own case for this theory.

That Plato's Atlantic island might have been located in the Caribbean was an intriguing possibility. As we know, in the *Timaeus* he tells us that it was situated within easy reach of "other islands" which acted like stepping stones for ancient voyagers wishing to reach "the opposite continent," or the American mainland. Such terminology could not describe the island chains of the Caribbean more accurately.... What we can also say is that up until around 5,000 years ago a great many of the Bahaman islands formed part of two enormous landmasses known as the Great and Little Bahama Banks, which were gradually submerged as the sea level rose following the melting of the ice fields at the end of the glacial age. Hydrographic surveys of the largest of these underwater platforms, the Great Bahama Bank, have indicated that this inundation process began as early as ca. 8000 B.C. and continued through until ca. 3000 B.C. Very slowly this whole landmass was flooded by the rising sea level to leave the many thousands of islands and cays which make up the Bahaman archipelago today. Similar processes resulted in the drowning of other low-lying regions in the Caribbean, some much quicker than others.

the central Mediterranean Sea), and the North Sea were also suggested. Candidates in the Middle East included Iran and Arabia. Even more exotic were theories that Atlantis was really Ceylon (an island off the coast of India), the Crimea (a peninsula in southern Russia), Mongolia, Brazil, Australia, the Arctic, and the Antarctic. Advocates for each of these locales advanced what they viewed as credible supporting evidence. But since only one of these theories can be correct (and possibly none are), the vast majority of this so-called proof is suspect from the start.

The Case Against the Atlantic

Putting the exact site of Atlantis aside for a moment, one line of evidence does strongly support the overall claim that Atlantis was situated someplace other than the Atlantic Ocean. In the twentieth century, geologists, oceanographers, and other scientists made important discoveries about the Atlantic seabed. The evidence they collected makes the idea of a continent sinking there in the recent past seem close to impossible. The case made *for* the Atlantic by Donnelly and many others was that only the plains and low hills of Atlantis had completely disappeared from view; the tops of the highest mountains, they argued, still protruded from the ocean's surface in the form of islands. As one Atlantologist states:

> Just as solitary church spires remain above the water when a dam is responsible for flooding a town, so only a few peaks of Atlantis rise above the surface today. The Azores, Madeira, Canary, and Cape Verde Islands, all of whose rocky sides slope straight down to the ocean floor without underwater platforms, were once mountain tops in Atlantis. Mount Atlas was the steepest, most massive mountain of the Atlantis range. Today it is called Pico Alto and is in the Azores Islands. Eruptions from this tall step

Pico Alto (background) in the Azores is believed by some to have been the highest mountain of the supposedly sunken continent of Atlantis.

volcano built Pico Alto higher and higher into a series of terraces before the sea consumed Atlantis.[26]

The trouble with this view is that it is totally unsupported by the geological evidence. Scientists now know that the basins of the oceans (as well as the continents) lie on huge plates that move very slowly across the Earth. This phenomenon is known as plate tectonics. Two of the plates meet in a ridge in the center of the Atlantic seabed, which is slowly being widened from the action of semiliquid rock rising from below the plates and pushing them apart. The thickness of the seabed formed in this manner averages about fifteen miles, the same as in the other ocean basins. By contrast, the thickness of the crust forming the continents averages thirty miles. If a continent had existed in the Atlantic and collapsed, the seabed should be much

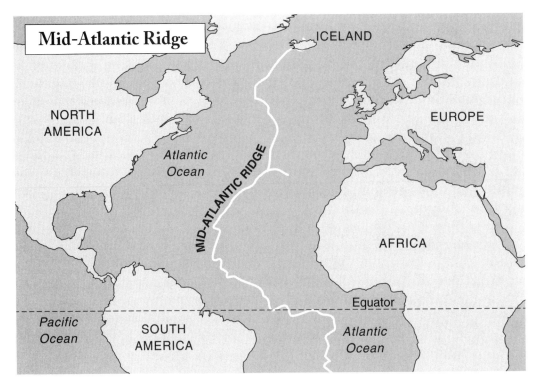

Mid-Atlantic Ridge

ICELAND

NORTH AMERICA

EUROPE

Atlantic Ocean

MID-ATLANTIC RIDGE

AFRICA

Equator

Pacific Ocean

SOUTH AMERICA

Atlantic Ocean

thicker than it is. Furthermore, cores (samples) taken from the seabed indicate no recent history of violent activity, as would have accompanied a sinking continent. The cores also show that the Atlantic ridge has not been above the water's surface for millions of years, if ever. If the ridge "was ever exposed," noted scientist Rachel Carson writes,

> it must have been at a time long before there were men to populate . . . an Atlantis. Some of the cores taken from the ridge show a continuous series of sediments typical of open oceans, far from land, running back to a period some 60 million years ago. And man, even the most primitive type, has appeared only within the past million years.[27]

Some geologists have also pointed out that, if a continent had sunk into the Atlantic in the recent past, the disaster would have generated large-scale destruction around the world. Monstrous waves would have rushed inland for many miles, crushing cities and forests and dramatically reshaping hills and shorelines. Physical evidence for such upheaval would be easily detectable today, yet no such evidence has been found.

The Lost Continent in Africa?

Atlantologists and other searchers are almost certainly right, therefore, to look for the lost continent somewhere beyond the Atlantic. For the most part, this means abandoning the notion of a large landmass suddenly sinking into a sea. The majority of the alternative theories about Atlantis suggest that it was an island or part of a continent that still exists, and that, over time, the memory of a localized flood or other disaster in the area became exaggerated to continental proportions.

One such disaster that some have cited for the demise of Atlantis occurred in North Africa. Reliable evidence shows that much of the Sahara Desert was well watered and fertile until only a few thousand years ago. It is probable, therefore, that the region once supported a larger human population than it does now, and that local farms and villages were abandoned as the climate rapidly became drier.

In fact, the idea that Atlantis was located in the Sahara Desert or other parts of North Africa was popular in the early twentieth century and is still believed in some quarters. In 1929, a book titled *Mysterious Sahara* was published by a European, Count Prorok, who claimed that he had found the skeleton of a prominent Atlantean in the Sahara. The skeleton turned out to be that of a modern native of the region, however. German geologist Paul Borchard claimed that Atlantis was in Tunisia, citing as evidence a ruined fortress that he believed was Atlantean in origin. But closer scrutiny by trained archaeologists later showed that the structure was Roman. Another North African theory was advanced by Frenchman Claude Roux, who held that the mountains of Morocco and Algeria had once been partially surrounded by an inlet of the Mediterranean Sea. This peninsula was the home of the fabled Atlanteans, he said, until the sea receded and the surrounding lands dried up.

Still another theory placing Atlantis in Africa, only much farther south, was that of German explorer Leo Frobenius. In the 1920s he claimed that the lost continent was not a continent at all, but the land inhabited by the Yoruba tribe (now Nigeria), on the western coast of Africa near the equator. The region had lush vegetation and elephants, like the ones mentioned by Plato, Frobenius noted. Also, says L. Sprague de Camp, Frobenius

> equated the Nigerian god Olokon [who in a myth flooded the land in the dim past] with Poseidon [cited by Plato as the creator of Atlantean civilization], and pointed out that the land had been the home of powerful maritime nations. . . . He also convinced himself that Yoruba culture contained many non-African elements.[28]

Since Frobenius's day, scholars have shown that the large nations and empires he attributed to the Yoruba were much

The seemingly endless dunes of the Sahara Desert were once fertile plains. Some Atlantologists believe Atlantis was located there.

smaller, localized city-states and kingdoms. Also, the cultural heyday of these states—dated to between A.D. 850 and 1350—was more than a thousand years after Plato introduced the Atlantis legend.

Atlantis in the North?

No less intriguing and perhaps more plausible than the African theories about Atlantis is one that locates it in the North Sea, the waterway bordered by the coasts of Britain, Denmark, and Scandinavia. Among the first writers to advance the North Sea hypothesis was Rachel Carson in her acclaimed 1951 book, *The Sea Around Us.* Carson draws attention to the Dogger Bank, lying between Britain and Denmark. A few thousand years ago, she points out, this shallow fishing area, about 160 miles long and 60 miles wide, was dry land. It had emerged from the sea during the previous ice age (during which the advance of glaciers caused sea levels to drop worldwide). "It was a low, wet land, covered with peat bogs," she writes. "Then, little by little the forests from the neighboring high lands must have moved in," and animals and people "moved down from the mainland and became established on this land recently won from the sea."[29]

Carson does not attempt to estimate how advanced the civilization of the Dogger Bank became or whether it interacted with the Mediterranean peoples to the south. She concentrates instead on the known fact that the young island and whatever civilization it possessed were eventually lost to the sea. The glaciers retreated and sea levels slowly rose, she writes.

> Finally, the sea covered the island, claiming the land and all its life. As for the men who escaped, perhaps in their primitive way they communicated this story to other men, who passed it down to others through the ages, until it became fixed in the

memory of the race. . . . And so the legend of a sinking continent might have been born.[30]

Another twist on the North Sea theory came in the 1979 book *Atlantis of the North*, by Jürgen Spanuth, a German clergyman. Spanuth agreed that the legend of Atlantis passed on by the Egyptians and Greeks was a distorted memory of a lost land in the North Sea; however, he placed that land south of the Dogger Bank, in the area of the small island of Heligoland. According to this view, the Atlanteans occupied this and some nearby islands, including Basileia, which sank into the sea in ancient times and thereby gave rise to the story of Atlantis's demise.

One strength of the North Sea scenario is that it places Atlantis relatively near the eastern Mediterranean. So, as Carson suggests, a folk memory of its disappearance could have filtered through Europe and eventually reached the Egyptians and Greeks, who recorded the Atlantis story. The theories involving Africa, Malta, France, Portugal, and Arabia also place Atlantis close enough to the eastern Mediterranean to make it believable that the Egyptian priests, Solon, and Plato could have heard about both its culture and its destruction.

The Fringe of Believability

In contrast, in ancient times, Atlantis candidates such as Brazil, Australia, Ceylon, and Mongolia were far removed from the European-Mediterranean "known world." Archaeologists have shown that their cultures were relatively primitive in the ages preceding Plato's Greece and had no contact with the Mediterranean sphere. So, it is highly improbable that any accounts of local wars or disasters in these distant regions could have reached the early Egyptians and Greeks.

If the ideas of a Mongolian or Australian Atlantis approach the fringe of believability, a number of other

The North Sea Hypothesis

Noted scientist Rachel Carson wrote briefly about Atlantis in her popular book *The Sea Around Us*. In this excerpt, she discusses the rising and sinking of the North Sea's Dogger Bank and how it might be related to the Atlantis legend.

During the Pleistocene [geologic age lasting from about 2 million to 11,000 B.C.], when immense quantities of water were withdrawn from the ocean and locked up in the glaciers, the floor of the North Sea emerged and for a time became land. It was a low, wet land, covered with peat bogs; then little by little the forests from the neighboring high lands . . . moved in. . . . Animals moved down from the mainland and became established on this land recently won from the sea. There were bears and wolves and hyenas, the wild ox, the bison, the woolly rhinoceros, and the mammoth. Primitive men moved through the forests, carrying crude stone instruments; they stalked deer and other game. . . . Then as the glaciers began to retreat and floods from the melting ice poured into the sea and raised its level, this land became an island. Probably the men escaped to the mainland before the intervening channel had become too wide, leaving their stone implements behind. But most of the animals remained . . . and little by little their island shrank, and food became more and more scarce, but there was no escape. Finally the sea covered the island, claiming the land and all its life. As for the men who escaped, perhaps in their primitive way they communicated this story to other men, who passed it down to others through the ages, until it became fixed in the memory of the race.

Environmentalist Rachel Carson proposed that the rising and sinking of the North Sea may have inspired the myth of Atlantis.

theories proposed about the lost continent are firmly on that fringe. Edgar Cayce's claims that Atlantis had airplanes and that many people today are reincarnated Atlanteans is a case in point. Another example is the notion that the mysterious force that allegedly causes ships and planes to disappear in the so-called Bermuda Triangle (in the southwestern Atlantic) also destroyed Atlantis. Charles Berlitz, who wrote the now famous 1974 book *The Bermuda Triangle*, writes in his 1984 work, *Atlantis: The Eighth Continent:*

> A recent theory suggests [that] sudden leaks or tears within the gas domes on the . . . continental shelves within the Triangle . . . cause great clouds of hydrogen gas to pour out. . . . When this gas comes to the surface, it [causes] surface ships to subside into it and sink. . . . This theory . . . emphasizes the constant changes and stresses of the seafloor, which may have caused or been the result of the catastrophe that overwhelmed Atlantis.[31]

Berlitz does not say who proposed this theory and gives no further details or analysis to support it. Moreover, not a shred of evidence has been found to confirm that bubbles of hydrogen gas have caused ships to sink in the Bermuda Triangle. Nor do any reputable geologists think that this mechanism could cause a large landmass to subside into the sea. (Berlitz's theory also loses credibility for claiming that a large sunken landmass lies at the bottom of the Atlantic, which scientists have shown is not the case.)

Visitors from the Heavens?

Even more outlandish are claims that, wherever Atlantis might have been, extraterrestrials (beings from other worlds) helped build it. Typical of this genre is Atlantologist Shirley Andrews's book, *Atlantis: Insights from a Lost Civilization*, in which she writes:

Study of prehistory points to visitors from the heavens whose advice enabled primitive peoples to improve their way of life relatively quickly. Amazing stone constructions attest to the worldwide influence of unknown engineers and builders with sophisticated techniques and skills. Plato's description of the architecture of the [metropolis of Atlantis] resembles the glorious cities of [ancient Mesopotamia, Central America, and southeast Asia]. As contemporary scientists are groping in the dark, attempting to explain how these anomalies came to be, they might consider the possibility that advice from friendly extraterrestrials was instrumental in their construction. Edgar Cayce's portrayal of the Atlanteans' use of a huge crystal to obtain energy from the sun and their varied means of transportation become more plausible if we surmise that visitors from space assisted them.[32]

Was Poseidon an Extraterrestrial?

In this excerpt from Shirley Andrews's recent book, *Atlantis: Insights from a Lost Civilization*, she asserts that Poseidon, patron of Atlantis, and other ancient gods were actually extraterrestrials (an allegation for which she provides no compelling evidence).

In ancient times, visitors from outer space to our planet were openly acknowledged and discussed, just as they are in some places in the world today. Plato describes the god Poseidon settling in Atlantis and marrying a mortal woman who bore many children. The theory that Poseidon was an extraterrestrial correlates with the descriptions in the Bible of "the sons of God who bred with the daughters of men." The Bible says these renowned men of pre-Christian times were "mighty." Poseidon's superhuman feats as he constructed his home, dug huge canals, and excavated for the City of the Golden Gates correlate with this description. Edgar Cayce matter-of-factly mentions extraterrestrials in his readings. In 1938, he described vehicles coming to the Earth during the late Atlantean period, whose occupants warned of the impending destruction of Atlantis.

These claims are unwarranted. First, study of early human societies by reputable scholars does not point to "visitors from the heavens." Archaeologists and other experts have repeatedly and conclusively demonstrated that all of the ancient monuments, from the Egyptian pyramids to the Great Wall of China, were constructed by people using simple tools, abundant manpower, and human ingenuity. Second, the fact that cities around the ancient world had similar architectural features suggests only that humans usually meet similar needs and solve similar problems in similar ways. Andrews' citation of Cayce's claims is also misguided. Credible scientific or historical research does not use one unsubstantiated theory to support another.

If discussion of Atlantis were limited to these and other fringe theories of Atlantis, as Richard Ellis says, "the post-Plato literature on Atlantis would long ago have been relegated to the 'Quacks and Lunatics' section of the library." In contrast, respected oceanographers, geologists, archaeologists, and other scholars prefer "a different sort of inquiry, one in which we examine the data as well as the interpretations in the light of science."[33] This is the method Rachel Carson used on a small scale in examining the North Sea theory. The Atlantis scenario that ended up attracting the attention and gaining the approval of a majority of classical scholars has employed this same method on a much larger scale. As it turned out, this theory places the lost continent much closer to home than any of the others—to Plato's home, that is.

The Atlantean Empire and Minoan Crete

During the twentieth century, while both Atlantologists and scientists looked around the globe for possible locations for Atlantis, a handful of classical scholars began to suspect these searchers were on the wrong track. Instead, the scholars suggested, the object of the famous legend lay much closer to homelands of the original sources, Egypt and Greece. Plato's story was as much about Athens as about Atlantis, they pointed out. After all, the centerpiece of the tale was a war between these two ancient states.

More importantly, the scholars asked, was it credible that the Bronze Age city of Athens would engage in a conflict with a power centered more than a thousand miles to the west? The Bronze Age, the stage of human culture featuring the use of tools and weapons made of bronze, lasted from about 3000 to 1100 B.C. in Europe and the Aegean region. In that era, which was more primitive than Plato's, Athens was a tiny kingdom in southeastern Greece and was largely preoccupied with rivalries with other small, Greek kingdoms. These scholars felt it was unlikely that Bronze Age Athens would have had either the inclination or the resources to fight a war against a foreign empire so far from home. This line of reasoning led to the proposal that the story of Atlantis was a distorted remembrance of an island empire located within the Greek sphere itself, specifically in the Aegean islands.

Theseus's Expedition to Crete

The first logical question these scholars asked was whether there had been a war in early Greek history in which the Athenians had defeated an aggressive island empire. And, in fact, just such a war is described in Greek mythology. In the famous tale of the Athenian hero Theseus, the large Greek island of Crete (lying about 190 miles southeast of Athens) held sway over a powerful maritime empire. The rulers of the Cretan city of Knossos, in northern Crete, intimidated the weaker Greek mainlanders. Each year these rulers demanded and received from Athens a ransom consisting of fourteen young men and women. The captives were taken to the Labyrinth, a huge building comprising a veritable maze of rooms and corridors. There, they

Theseus Defeats the Cretans

This is part of Plutarch's account of Theseus's exploits in Crete (from his *Life of Theseus*, as translated by Ian Scott-Kilvert in *The Rise and Fall of Athens*).

When the ships were ready he set out, taking Daedalus [a Greek who had built the Labyrinth for the Cretan king and then escaped from Crete] and a number of Cretan exiles as his guides. The Cretans had no warning of his movements and supposed that the oncoming fleet was friendly, so that Theseus was able to seize the har-

bor, disembark his men, and reach Knossos before his arrival was discovered. There he fought a battle at the gates of the Labyrinth and killed Deucalion [son of the Cretan king] and his bodyguard. As Ariadne [the Cretan king's daughter] now succeeded to the throne, he made a truce with her, recovered the young Athenians, and concluded a pact of friendship between the Athenians and the Cretans, who swore that they would never in the future begin a war with Athens.

This Greek amphora depicts Theseus slaying the Minotaur. Classical scholars have noted similarities between the Minoan civilization of Crete and Plato's description of Atlantis.

became the unfortunate victims of the Minotaur, a creature half-man and half-bull.

To stop this outrage, Theseus eventually led a naval expedition against Crete. According to Plutarch, "When the ships were ready, he set out" and, on reaching northern Crete, he "was able to seize the harbor, disembark his men, and reach Knossos before his arrival was discovered." Theseus and his men "fought a battle at the gates of the Labyrinth," after which he entered the maze and slew the Minotaur. After that, the Cretans "swore that they would never in the future begin a war with Athens."[34]

Until the dawn of the twentieth century, historians and other scholars viewed this myth as nothing more than a fable. Then, in 1900, British archaeologist Sir Arthur Evans began uncovering a huge, palacelike structure at Knossos. It contained hundreds of rooms and corridors on multiple levels, like the Labyrinth in the myth. Soon, other similar palaces were discovered elsewhere in Crete, revealing a powerful, Bronze Age, maritime empire exactly like the mythical one. (It later became clear that these so-called palaces were religious temples and administrative centers as well as royal residences.) Scholars dubbed this ancient civilization Minoan after Minos, a legendary Cretan king. Also as in the myth, Knossos showed signs of burning and other destruction; and excavators found evidence that invaders from the mainland had been the culprits.

The similarities between the Minoans and mythical Cretans were not all that scholars noticed. In 1909, K.T. Frost, of Queen's University in Belfast, reviewed recent findings in Crete and saw close parallels between the Minoans and Plato's Atlanteans. In an article for the *Times* of London, he wrote:

> As a political and commercial force . . . Knossos and its allied cities were swept away just when they seemed strongest and safest. It was as if the whole kingdom had sunk into the sea, as if the tale of Atlantis were true. . . . If the account of Atlantis be compared with the history of Crete and her relationship with Greece and Egypt, it seems almost certain that here we have an echo of the Minoans. . . . The whole description of Atlantis which is given in the *Timaeus* and the *Critias* has features so thoroughly Minoan that even Plato could not have invented so many unsuspected facts.[35]

Solon in Egypt

In this excerpt from his biography of Solon (translated by Ian Scott-Kilvert in *The Rise and Fall of Athens*), Plutarch describes the Greek lawgiver's stay in Egypt and his acquisition of the Atlantis story.

He went first of all to Egypt and stayed for a while, as he mentions himself. . . . He also spent some time studying and discussing philosophy with Psenophis of Heliopolis and Sonchis of Saïs, who were the most learned of the Egyptian priests. According to Plato it was from them that he heard the legend of the lost continent of Atlantis, which he tried to introduce to the Greeks in the form of a poem. . . . He finally abandoned [the poem], however, not, as Plato suggests, for lack of time, but rather because of his age and his fear that the task would be too much for him.

The Wrong Pillars

One obvious parallel that Frost and others noted between Minoan Crete and Atlantis came from Plato's description of the lands dominated by the Atlantean empire. "Now in this island of Atlantis," Plato writes, "there was a great and wonderful empire which had rule over the whole island and several others, and over parts of the continent."[36] In Frost's words, "This sentence describes the political status of Knossos . . . concisely."[37] Indeed, archaeology has shown that the Minoans dominated Crete, the nearby islands, and parts of mainland Greece (which itself is part of the larger continent of Europe).

At first glance, it would seem that placing the Atlantean empire this close to Greece contradicts Plato's assertion that Atlantis lay in the Atlantic Ocean. His exact words are: "There was an island situated in front of the straits which are by you [i.e., the Greeks] called the Pillars of Heracles."[38] It is true that this was the name given by the Greeks to the Strait of Gibraltar, which would imply an island lying beyond the strait, in the Atlantic. However, this was only one geographic site labeled the Pillars of Heracles by the Greeks. Before about 600 B.C. (Solon's era), the two southernmost peninsulas of mainland Greece—Cape Tainaron and Cape Malea—bore that same name. A glance at a map of the region reveals that these peninsulas point directly at nearby western Crete. "To the Greeks," Rodney Castleden points out, "a large island with one end just outside the Pillars of Heracles could only have meant Crete."[39] Thus, the Egyptian priests and perhaps Solon had the closer pillars in mind, while Plato, who lived centuries later, assumed it was the more distant ones. That explains why he placed the island empire in the Atlantic.

Another close parallel between Minoan Crete and Atlantis is that each had a large, fertile plain. According to Plato, Atlantis's plain was "surrounded by mountains which descended towards the sea; it was smooth and even, and of an oblong shape. . . . This part of the island looked towards the south, and was sheltered from the north [winds]."[40] Crete's central plain of Mesara is also oblong, that is, longer than it is wide; and it, too, is sheltered from the north winds by a range of mountains.

To be fertile, the plain would have needed abundant sunshine. And, in the *Critias*, Plato describes Atlantis as having two seasons, a warm, dry summer and a rainy winter (which implies a short, mild winter). This is a classic description of the Mediterranean climate enjoyed by southern Greece and the Aegean Islands. This fact, alone, definitely places Atlantis in the Mediterranean; for, if it had been a continent in the midst of the Atlantic, its climate, including that of its central plain, would be markedly different.

Still another similarity between the Minoan and Atlantean empires is the manner in which they were administered. Plato says that Poseidon had ten sons and assigned each of them a portion of the empire. Moreover, all were equal in status, with the exception of one who held some kind of prestige or authority over the others, a sort of head king. Little is known about Minoan government and administration, but four large palace centers existed on Crete—at Knossos, Mallia (also on the north coast), Kato Zakro (in the east), and Phaistos (in the south)—along with a smaller one at Hagia Triada (in the south). Each of these centers seems to have had a local ruler who was equal in rank to the others but who also recognized the king of Knossos as the general overlord. When the rulers of some of the major Minoan colonies on nearby islands are factored in, the resulting political situation is remarkably like the one described in the *Critias*.

The respective regions controlled by these local rulers had names, some of which have been preserved in surviving Cretan writings. The name for the central portion of the island was Atlunus, which raises an intriguing possibility. During the Bronze Age, the Egyptians carried on long-distance trade with the Minoans, whom they called the Keftiu. (Wall paintings of Keftiu, easily identifiable as Minoans by their dress, have been found in Egypt.) Many of these traders might have identified their homeland as Atlunus. When Cretan civilization fell and trade ceased between the two countries, Egyptian priests would have recorded the sudden end of the faraway island empire of Atlunus; and, as this story was told and retold during the many centuries that followed, Atlunus became Atlantis. (An alternate view is that the Egyptians continued to call Crete Keftiu, meaning "land with a pillar that holds up the sky"; and it was Plato who named it Atlantis after Atlas, the mythological character who held up the sky.)[41]

A Building Marvelous to Behold

One of the most striking parallels between Atlantis and Minoan Crete is the similarity between the temple of Poseidon in the Atlantean metropolis and the palace center at Knossos. Here is part of Plato's description of the Atlantean version:

> They built the palace . . . which they continued to ornament in successive generations, every king surpassing the one who went before him to the utmost of his power, until they made the building a marvel to behold for size and for beauty. . . . Here was Poseidon's own temple which was a stadium [about six hundred feet] in length, and half a stadium in width, and of a proportionate height, having a strange barbaric appearance. . . . They had fountains, one of cold and another of hot water, in gracious plenty flowing. . . . Also they made cisterns, some open to the heavens, others roofed over, to be used in winter as warm baths; there were the kings' baths, and the baths of private persons, which were kept apart; and there were separate baths for women . . . and to each of them they gave as much adornment as was suitable.[42]

First, the dimensions of Poseidon's edifice—six hundred by three hundred feet—roughly match those of the palace of Knossos, which is about six hundred feet on a side. Second, Plato's claim that successive generations of Atlanteans created a building that was "a marvel to behold for size" and had "a strange barbaric appearance" is a perfect description of the Knossos palace. "By ancient standards," Castleden writes, the Minoan Labyrinth

> was a lofty building. The East Wing . . . was four or five stories high. . . . The labyrinth would have looked strange and barbaric to foreigners, and also

This section of the palace-center at Knossos shows some of the complex, split-level architecture reminiscent of the Atlantean palace described by Plato.

to those who saw its ruins in later times. The building lacked symmetry. . . . Doors were positioned near the corners of rooms as if to provoke curiosity. . . . Corridors and stairs twisted and turned, roof lines rose and fell. . . . It was built on totally different lines from the temples of [Greece's] classical period [i.e., Plato's era]. . . . To the classical Greeks it was very strange, outlandish, and foreign.[43]

Plato's description of cisterns (tanks for catching rainwater) and comfortable bathrooms brings to mind the incredibly advanced plumbing facilities at Knossos. Sophisticated systems of clay pipes and drains brought clean water into the baths and carried away dirty water and wastes. As classical scholar J.V. Luce says:

The excellence and "modernity" of the plumbing and drainage system of the palace of Minos has always excited admiring comment. The queen's [suite] had its own separate bathroom and toilet. On the northeast corner of the palace, an elaborate series of runnels [water channels] . . . carried the run-off of rain water through two small settling tanks to a large cistern. These details . . . seem to provide quite strong circumstantial evidence for identifying Atlantis with Crete.[44]

Identical Bull Rituals

Even more striking is that both the Atlantean temple and Minoan palace were religious centers featuring a bull cult, as both peoples had the same reverence for bulls. "There were bulls who had the range of the temple of Poseidon,"[45] Plato writes. And, at Knossos, wall paintings and other

This Minoan mural depicts a man leaping over a bull. Some scholars have noted that both Atlantis and Minoan Crete shared a special reverence for the bull.

evidence show that bulls were brought inside the palace center, where they became part of elaborate rituals. (Some priests likely wore bull masks, giving rise to the legend of the Minotaur.) These rituals included games, in which young men and women leapt over the bulls' backs, and presumably sacrifice. (No paintings of actual sacrifice have yet been found in the palace, but scholars believe that the Minoans, like other ancient peoples, sacrificed sacred animals to their gods.)

Also, the way the bulls were hunted in Atlantis and Minoan Crete is identical. According to Plato, the Atlanteans "hunted the bulls without weapons but with staves [wooden sticks] and nooses." And, after the animals were sacrificed, the kings "filled a bowl of wine and cast in a clot of [bull's] blood for each of them" and then "drew [wine] from the bowl in golden cups."[46] In the early years of the twentieth century, two Minoan golden goblets (known as the Vapheio cups) were discovered. Carved on their sides is a perfectly preserved scene of men hunting bulls with sticks and nooses. Frost wrote, in 1909:

> Plato's words exactly describe the scenes on the famous Vapheio cups, which certainly represent catching wild bulls for the Minoan [bull ritual], which, as we know from the palace itself, differed from all others which the world has seen exactly in the point which Plato emphasizes—namely that no weapons were used.[47]

Homer's Scheria

The fact that Plato's account includes these and other details about Minoan civilization naturally raises the question of whether he and other Greeks of his day knew about the Minoans. To answer this question, it is necessary to consider the ultimate fate of Minoan Crete. In the late 1400s B.C., the Greek mainlanders (whom modern scholars call the Mycenaeans) overran the Minoan towns and palace centers. The Mycenaeans then controlled the surrounding islands and seaways until the Bronze Age came to a shattering close between 1200 and 1100 B.C. In an upheaval that is still not fully understood, towns and palaces across Greece and parts of the Middle East were destroyed, never to be rebuilt. Greece then entered a dark age in which writing and many other aspects of culture disappeared. Over time, people steadily forgot their heritage, and the major figures and events of the Minoan-Mycenaean world faded into the realm of legend.

Born many centuries later, Plato and his contemporaries did not know who had built the Bronze Age structures whose decayed ruins could still be seen in some places. So, he did not know about the Minoans, and that is why he did not correlate Atlantis with Crete. It appears that Plato got some of his information about the lost continent from the account of the Egyptian priests. But it seems strange that people in faraway Egypt would possess the only mythical account of Greece's Bronze Age civilization. Indeed, it stands to reason that an oral tradition with details in general agreement with the Egyptian version would have been preserved in Greece itself.

Most classical scholars now believe that just such an oral tradition *was* preserved in Greece. From this legend, they propose, the Greek bard Homer drew inspiration for his descriptions of the fabulous island of Scheria (or Phaeacia) in his epic poem the *Odyssey*. (In the poem, Scheria is one of the lands visited by the Greek hero Odysseus in his wanderings following the Trojan War.) Scheria had thirteen kings, with one wielding authority over the others, similar to Atlantis's ten kings, one of whom was paramount; moreover, Scheria's rulers, like the Atlantean kings, claimed descent from the god Poseidon. Also, both Scheria and Atlantis had a fertile central plain, complex harbors and docks, highly decorated temples dedi-

cated to Poseidon, and two freshwater springs. Overall, the detailed similarities among Homer's Scheria, Plato's Atlantis, Crete in the myth of Theseus, and the real Minoan Crete strongly suggest that all are one and the same place. And this seems to verify that the Egyptian account of Atlantis was based on real events in the Greek sphere.[48]

The architecture of Cretan buildings resembles the building designs described in Plato's account of Atlantis.

The Missing Detail

Frost and other scholars of the early twentieth century were certainly struck by these parallels, but one major parallel between Atlantis and Crete was still sorely lacking, namely, the sinking of Atlantis into the sea. Many minor details of Plato's account had seemingly been based loosely on fact; yet Crete was still very much intact above the waves, which suggested that one major detail of the story was wrong. Did the Egyptian priests, or Solon, or Plato simply make up the catastrophe?

The answer to this question began to emerge in the 1930s, when a young Greek archaeologist named Spyridon Marinatos made an intriguing discovery. He found that some giant stones from the wall of a Minoan structure in

Parallels Between Scheria and Atlantis

In his fascinating book about Atlantis, *The Flood from Heaven*, scholar Eberhard Zangger lists these parallels, among others, between the land of Scheria in the text of Homer's *Odyssey* and Atlantis in the text of Plato's *Critias*.

Scheria	Atlantis
"Our city is surrounded by high battlements; it has an excellent harbor on each side and is approached by a narrow causeway." "Odysseus marveled at the harbors with their well-founded ships, at the meeting-place of the sea-lords and at their long lofty walls, which were surmounted by palisades [battlements] and presented a wonderful sight."	"Beginning at the sea, they bored a channel and thus they made the entrance to it from the sea like that to a harbor by opening out a mouth large enough for the greatest ships to sail through and after crossing the three outer harbors, full of triremes [ships] and all the tackling that belongs to triremes. They erected towers and gates and the royal palace likewise was such as befitted the greatness of the kingdom, and equally befitted the splendor of the temples."
"The garden is served by two springs, one led in rills to all parts of the enclosure, while its fellow opposite, after providing a watering-place for the townsfolk, runs under the courtyard gate towards the great house [palace] itself."	"Bringing up from beneath the earth two springs of waters . . . [the Atlanteans] conducted [the outflowing water] to the sacred grove of Poseidon and by means of channels they led the water to the outer circles over against the bridges."
"Here is the people's meeting-place, built up on either side of the fine temple of Poseidon with blocks of quarried stone bedded deeply into the ground."	"In the center there stood a temple sacred to Cleito and Poseidon which was reserved as holy ground, and encircled with a wall and the stone they quarried beneath the central island all round."

Crete had been mysteriously displaced and dragged. He realized that this could only have been done by enormous amounts of water, probably a tsunami (sometimes called a tidal wave). Could this disaster have had some bearing on Plato's tale of Atlantis, he wondered? And if so, where had these great waves come from?

Chapter 5

Thera and the Blast That Shook History

The shroud of mystery surrounding the true identity of Atlantis began to be penetrated by K.T. Frost and a few other classical scholars working in the early twentieth century. They speculated that the memory of Minoan civilization and its Crete-centered empire had given rise to the legend of Atlantis, yet they had to admit that one major event in that legend—the island's submergence during a great catastrophe—did not have a Cretan parallel. Clearly, Crete had never sunk into the sea. It remained for a member of the next generation of scholars to explain this crucial element of the mystery.

That key player in the unfolding Atlantean-Minoan scenario was Spyridon Marinatos, a young Greek archaeologist who was fascinated by the continuing Minoan finds on Crete. In 1932, at the age of thirty-one, Marinatos traveled to Amnisos, on the island's northern coast. There he excavated two very ancient villas. Even more intriguing than these structures, however, was the evidence he found for an ancient catastrophe. Giant stone building blocks, each weighing many tons, had been lifted up and deposited hundreds of feet away, and thick layers of volcanic pumice (a light, porous form of dried lava) blanketed many parts of the area. He wrote in his published findings, in 1939:

> What really piqued [stimulated] my interest . . . were the curious positions of several huge stone blocks that had been torn from their foundations and strewn around the sea. . . . I found a building near the shore with its basement full of pumice. This fact I tentatively ascribed to a huge eruption of Thera, which geologists . . . thought had occurred [in the Bronze Age].[49]

The place mentioned by Marinatos, Thera, is a group of three small islands (one main island and two smaller ones) lying about seventy miles north of Crete's northern coast, almost directly north of Knossos. Thera, the main island's ancient name, is still used, although more people call it by its modern name, Santorini. An active volcano lies in the center of the bay, separating the three Theran islands.

Abundant evidence collected by geologists, archaeologists, and other scientists over the course of more than a century has shown that sometime, roughly between 1625 and 1500 B.C., this volcano erupted with enormous violence. Indeed, many scientists call it the largest natural disaster in recorded history. The eruption created monstrous tsunamis that devastated the surrounding islands, including Crete, and its effects were felt as far away as Palestine and Egypt. As Marinatos and other scholars eventually showed, Thera's great blast, likely, both changed the course of history and gave rise to the enduring legend of sunken Atlantis.

How Thera's Awesome Features Formed

The testimony of the great Bronze Age eruption is still written plainly for all to see in the topography of the Theran island group. Thera, the main island in the group, is shaped like a narrow crescent; its curving arms partially enclose a large, almost circular bay about six miles in diameter; the two other islands, Therasia and tiny Aspronisi, lie on the far side of the bay. Sailing into the bay, one immediately encounters an awesome sight. The inner side of Thera's crescent is made up of sheer cliffs that tower to a height of 1,200 feet in some places. A layer of volcanic ash and pumice from 60 to 150 feet deep rests on top of the cliffs (and lies beneath the soil across the whole island).

As geologists have shown, the circular bay, the cliffs, and most of the ash layers are remnants of the cataclysmic Bronze Age eruption. Before that disaster, the bay did not exist and the three islands in the group were joined together as one roughly circular island. In fact, the island's earliest name was Srongyle, meaning "the round one." Near the center of the island stood a massive volcano (with, perhaps, two or more separate cones) that tapered in a gradual, gentle slope toward sea level. It is worth recalling Plato's remark in the *Critias* that "in the center of the island [containing the Atlantean metropolis] there was a mountain not very high on any side."[50]

In the early stages of the eruption, the volcano spewed out huge amounts of ash, pumice, and other debris, some of which Marinatos later found at Amnisos, in Crete. Some geologic discoveries suggest that the eruption occurred in stages, each preceded by earthquakes. Considering this, it is not surprising that archaeologists have found evidence that most of the island's inhabitants departed

Why Plato Mentions No Volcano

Some people have objected to the Theran connection to the Atlantis legend because Plato does not say that Atlantis was destroyed by a volcanic eruption. In this tract from his book *Atlantis Destroyed*, scholar Rodney Castleden responds that no one in ancient times realized that the disappearance of central Thera was connected to the island's volcano.

Earthquakes centered on Thera were experienced over a large area in the Aegean and therefore could be reported and remembered by those who survived on the other island. . . . It would have been obvious to those sailing past the island after the catastrophe that its center had vanished. There may even have been some down-faulted blocks still remaining round the caldera walls to indicate how the island had fallen in. But no witnesses of the eruption itself can have lived to tell the tale. We can infer the progress of the eruption sequence in detail using modern techniques of archaeology and geology, but no one could have done that in the Bronze Age, or indeed in Plato's day.

before the climax of the disaster. No doubt, the successive earthquakes and rains of volcanic debris scared them off.

As it turned out, escape was a wise course of action. No one then living could have imagined that deep beneath Thera's volcanic cones a deadly chain of geologic events were nearing a truly shattering conclusion. The initial phases of the eruption had steadily emptied the vast magma chamber inside and beneath the volcano. (Magma is hot molten rock that sometimes rises from the depths of the Earth.) For ages, the magma within the chamber had supported the heavy volcanic cones and slopes above. But, when the chamber emptied, gravity had its way. The entire central portion of the island suddenly collapsed, forming a deep circular depression called a caldera. (The sheer cliffs on Thera's inner edge are the upper sections of the caldera's walls.) Seawater immediately rushed in to fill the void, and then rebounded with a fury, sending out tremendous tsunamis in all directions. Some of these waves rushed ashore on the northern coast of Crete and smashed into the buildings at Amnisos, dislodging the large building stones that Marinatos later discovered there.

Krakatoa as a Model for Thera

The remains of other ancient volcanic calderas can be seen all over the world. By 1883, geologists had studied these and pieced together a rough picture of how this special kind of eruption—a caldera formation—works. But they had never witnessed such an event to verify their theories. Then, early in 1883, the volcano on the small island of Krakatoa, in the narrow strait between the large islands of Java and Sumatra (in Indonesia), began to erupt. The event happened in stages, as the volcano disgorged ash and pumice at intervals. Finally, in August, the volcanic cone collapsed, creating a caldera and generating large sea waves.

It was this modern Krakatoan eruption that Marinatos used as a model for his emerging theory about the devastation of the Minoan sphere by Thera's Bronze Age eruption. By studying the extent of the devastation caused by

Some believe the Bronze Age volcanic eruption that formed the sheer cliffs of Thera (pictured) and sank much of the island gave rise to a legend of Atlantis's demise.

the more recent eruption, he reasoned, he could estimate the damage the ancient eruption had done. In his 1939 paper, he wrote:

> The island of Krakatoa is much smaller than Thera and the part of it that was submerged was about a quarter of the other (22.8 square km against 83 in Thera). . . . Vast quantities of pumice coated both the island [of Krakatoa] and a great part of the sea round about. . . . A tremendous roar accompanied the explosion [i.e., the final collapse] and was heard over 2,000 miles away—just one-twelfth of the earth's circumference. . . . But worst of all was a series of terrific waves which rose after the explosion. They were as much as 90 feet high, and broke with devastating force and speed against the coasts of Java and Sumatra. Where they struck a plain, they swept inland, and as far as [3,000 feet] inland they were still [45 feet] high. Whole towns, villages and woods were destroyed. . . . The amazing catastrophe cost over 36,000 lives.[51]

As Marinatos pointed out, the amount of material that collapsed in the Krakatoan disaster was only about a quarter of that which disappeared in the Theran eruption. This means that four times as much energy was generated at Thera. Also, the water lying between Thera and northern Crete is many times deeper than the water lying between Java and Sumatra. The size of a tsunami is determined not only by the amount of energy that generates it, but also by the depth of the water through which it travels. Simply put, the deeper the water, the bigger the waves. Thus, the waves that struck ancient Crete were much larger than the ones generated by Krakatoa, perhaps several hundred feet high. "The mud-brick upper stories of tall Cretan palaces and mansions could have suffered very severely," says J.V. Luce:

Upwards of 36,000 people perished within twenty-four hours on Java and Sumatra, and 290 towns and villages were destroyed. . . . I consider it a safe guess that the loss of life and damage to property were no less [on Crete]. They may well have been many times as great. . . . In addition to the effects of the blast and tidal waves . . . the hills and valleys of eastern Crete were covered to a considerable depth of ash fall-out. . . . We can envisage that the Minoans

This drawing depicts the eruption of Krakatoa in Indonesia in 1883. Thera's eruption was four times as powerful as the Krakatoan disaster.

of central and eastern Crete who escaped the waves may well have found much of their land uncultivable, their orchards destroyed . . . and their buildings flattened. This factor of fall-out could be the explanation for . . . the westward migration [of the Minoan population] which is clear from the archaeological evidence.[52]

The effects of the waves and ashfall also explain why Minoan civilization went into a fatal decline. Not only were large numbers of lives lost and farmland ruined, but most of the Minoans' ships, the mainstay of the maritime empire, must have been destroyed as well. Evidence shows that the Minoans did survive the catastrophe; they rebuilt many of the damaged structures and, no doubt, built more ships and partially replenished their population. But they were unable to make a total recovery before the Mycenaean warlords swept down from mainland Greece and overran them in the fifteenth century B.C.

Thera's Waves Remembered in Myths

The giant tsunamis generated by the Theran caldera formation swept through the Aegean Sea and inundated thousands of miles of low-lying coastlines. One would expect that these waves or the floods they created would be remembered in the folklore of the peoples of the region, just as the disaster was remembered in the legend of Atlantis. And this is, indeed, the case. Many of these legends involve Poseidon, the sea god said to have been Atlantis's patron. In a famous Athenian myth, for example, Poseidon and the goddess Athena have a contest for the patronage of Athens. When Athena wins, Poseidon loses his temper and floods the nearby countryside. In

a similar myth, Poseidon loses a contest to the goddess Hera and in his anger causes the sea to cover the Argive plain (in southeastern Greece). Also, the Greek biographer Plutarch mentions a folk tradition in which Poseidon sends a great wave to cover the countryside around Lycia (on the southeastern shore of the Aegean). In addition, the Greek historian Diodorus records that the people of the Aegean island of Rhodes had a tradition about a destructive tide that flooded their land; he also says that, in his own time, the people of the Aegean island of Samothrace still marked the floodline where, in a past age, some great sea waves had come to rest.

Two Islands Remembered As One

Thus, it became clear to scholars that the Bronze Age eruption of Thera had caused an island to sink into the sea, just as in Plato's tale of Atlantis. Yet two inconsistencies appeared to remain when factoring Thera into the Atlantean-Minoan scenario. First, Crete, with its fertile plain, and Thera, with its central mountain that was "not very high on any side," are two separate islands. True, Plato's account does describe the central mountain and the fertile plain as occupying different islands. The central hill was surrounded by circular zones of water, setting it apart from the larger portion of Atlantis that contained the plain. However, the splendid temple of Poseidon seems to have been a garbled memory of the palace of Knossos. How could one explain the contradiction that, in the legend, the temple lay on the smaller island, whereas, in reality, Knossos is on Crete, the larger island?

Marinatos and other researchers explained this apparent inconsistency in a simple and logical manner. The Egyptians, they said, who lived far away from the Aegean region, had only a muddled impression of the empire from which Minoan traders hailed. It contained many islands, most of which the Egyptians knew nothing about. So, after the Theran disaster, they mistakenly conflated, or combined, elements of separate islands into a single island. As Marinatos himself put it in a 1950 article titled "On the Atlantis Legend":

> The Egyptians heard about the sinking of an island, which was Thera, but this island, small and insignificant, was unknown to them. This event they transferred to the neighboring Crete, an island which was dreadfully struck [by a catastrophe] and with which they had lost contact suddenly.[53]

The second inconsistency concerned the nature of the civilization on Thera. For the Atlantean-Minoan-Theran theory to be valid, Thera had to have been inhabited by Minoans or, at least, by people who shared close cultural and economic ties with them. In 1967, Marinatos, by this time Greece's leading archaeologist, began excavating a site near Akrotiri, a village on Thera's southern coast. Before long, a Bronze Age Minoan town began to emerge from the ash layers some thirty-five centuries after it had been buried. Many streets filled with residences and shops, some two stories high, have since been uncovered, along with magnificent frescoes (wall paintings made on wet plaster) and other priceless artifacts. Moreover, evidence suggests that the town, most of which still lies buried, was very large and prosperous, and that a portion of it probably disappeared into the caldera when the volcano collapsed.

The Disaster Remembered in Legend

The event that swallowed up part of ancient Akrotiri and buried the rest of the town was a catastrophe of truly enormous proportions. It would be surprising if the memory of such a significant event was not preserved in surviving folklore and writings in Greece and other nearby regions. In fact, it seems certain that the effects of the eruption *were* memorialized. For example, the Greek poet Hesiod, who flourished about 700 B.C., recorded a well-known myth about the devastation wrought during a great battle between the god Zeus and a giant monster in the dim past. "The whole earth boiled and heaven and the sea," he wrote. "The great waves raged along the shore . . . and endless quakes arose. Great Earth groaned."[54] It is noteworthy that the huge waves, earthquakes, and loud groan, or roar, are not mentioned as separate events, but as part of the same event. And the largest event that could have produced such effects in the Greek sphere in the Bronze Age was the formation of Thera's caldera.

Another Greek legend, which involves Theseus and other characters from the Bronze Age, was committed to paper by the fifth-century Athenian playwright Euripides in his *Hippolytus*. A messenger tells Theseus:

> There is a stretch of shore that [faces] the Saronic Gulf. Here, from the ground a roar like Zeus's thunderclap came sounding heavy round us, terrible to hear. . . . And when we looked upon the foaming shores, we saw a monstrous wave towering up to the

This Minoan fresco shows two boys boxing. Thera's cataclysmic eruption and tsunami destroyed Minoan civilization thirty-five hundred years ago.

79

Thera and the War in Heaven

In his *Theogony*, the early Greek poet Hesiod, who was perhaps a much younger contemporary of Homer, described the mythical battle between Zeus, leader of the Olympian gods, and a giant monster called Typhon. Many scholars see in the passage (quoted here from Dorothea Wender's translation) a distorted memory of the Thera catastrophe.

> The earth rang terribly, broad heaven above, the sea, and Ocean's streams and Tartarus [a region of the Underworld] resounded. As the lord arose, mighty Olympus shook beneath the immortal feet, and Earth gave out a groan. The purple sea was seized by heat from both, from thunder and from lightning, and from fire the monster bore—the burning hurricane and blazing thunderbolt. The whole earth boiled and heaven and the sea. The great

waves raged along the shore, at the immortal's charge, and endless quakes arose. . . . Great Earth groaned. A flame leaped from the lightning-blasted lord, when he was struck, on the jagged mountainside. Great earth was widely scorched by the awful blast and melted.

The myth of the battle between Zeus (top left) and Typhon (top right) may be a distorted memory of the destruction of Thera.

sky. . . . Swelling up and surging onward, with all around [it] a mass of foam . . . it neared the shore.[55]

The Saronic Gulf lies along the southeastern coast of the Greek mainland, directly facing Thera. This is exactly how a Theran-generated tsunami would have looked to someone standing on high ground overlooking the gulf. Similar legends of great waves and floods abound in the folklore of ancient peoples living along the coasts of the Aegean and eastern Mediterranean.

In Egypt, too, some ancient legends and writings seem to be connected with the Theran disaster. One, of course, is the account of Atlantis that Plato used in his dialogues. It appears to have been based on later reports given to the Egyptians by foreign merchants or other travelers who had witnessed some of the devastation in the Aegean region. Another Egyptian account describes the effects of the calamity in Egypt itself. Such effects would surely have been inevitable. The tsunamis, greatly reduced in size after a long journey, would have struck the country's northern coast, and the airborne ash would have caused the sky to grow dark across much of the eastern Mediterranean basin. An inscription by the pharaoh Ahmose (who reigned 1550–1525 B.C.) reads, in part:

> The gods expressed their discontent. . . . A tempest
> . . . caused darkness in the western region [i.e., the
> part of Egypt lying closest to the Aegean]. The sky
> was unleashed . . . more than the roar of the crowd.
> . . . Houses and shelters [from local villages destroyed
> by the waves] were floating on the water . . . for
> days.[56]

As Marinatos pointed out, the Egyptians knew nothing about the tiny island of Thera. They had no idea that the waves, darkness, and loud roars that reached their own land had been generated in the distant Aegean. Their stories about the disaster, along with others from many lands, soon became disconnected fragments floating in a vast sea of intermingled history and myth. Many long centuries came and went until, finally, Frost, Marinatos, and other modern scholars began to search for the truth. Through logic, ingenuity, patience, and plain hard work, they managed to reassemble the puzzle pieces and solve the mystery of lost Atlantis at last.

Chapter 6

Myths as Memories: The Making of a Legend

The research and educated speculation of a number of classical scholars and scientists over the course of the twentieth century established an extremely strong case for the origins of the legend of Atlantis. In their view, now widely (though not universally) accepted, that legend was a garbled recollection of the Minoan empire and Thera eruption. Based on their studies, it is now possible to piece together a credible scenario of what happened long ago in the Greek Bronze Age. It is the story of a prosperous maritime empire, a great catastrophe that struck it suddenly, and the process by which the memory of these things was transformed into the myth of Atlantis.

Prelude to Catastrophe

Actually, the dramatic and convoluted story of Atlantis's origins begins long before the Bronze Age, in the dim past when no humans lived on the Aegean Islands. Millions of years ago, a group of small, rocky islands existed in the spot now occupied by Thera. Then, a volcano steadily grew from below, eventually rising above the water's surface and filling in the spaces between the rocky islands. The debris from many successive eruptions accumulated and spread outward until there was one, almost perfectly round island on the spot. From time to time, during the largest eruptions, part of the island collapsed, forming small calderas. Geologic evidence suggests that a round-shaped bay formed this way in the island's southwest sector about 54,000 B.C. (This bay still existed in the early Bronze Age and eventually became part of the much larger caldera seen today.)

Time passed and successive eruptions produced two or more volcanic cones in the northern half of the island. But long periods of calm prevailed between eruptions. During these quiet stretches, trees, vines, and other vegetation flourished in the rich volcanic soil, making the place very inviting to the first human settlers. Archaeological evidence suggests that they arrived about 4500 B.C., probably from the Greek mainland. It makes sense that they came during one of the quiet periods between eruptions and had no notion of the danger posed by the then-picturesque mountains lying north of the pleasant southern bay.

In the centuries that followed, the early Therans erected villages. From time to time, earthquakes caused significant damage, but the villages were always rebuilt. And at least one, which grew where modern Akrotiri is now situated, became a large, prosperous town. Then, a really large earthquake struck circa 1950 B.C. Again, the Therans rebuilt. Afterward, the evidence shows, they began to have strong contacts with Crete, where a vibrant, culturally advanced people, the Minoans, had established their own prosperous communities.

For years, the Therans and Minoans traded with each other and the former felt the cultural influence of the latter.

Excavated Minoan buildings on Thera are covered with volcanic ash. The eruption of Thera was audible as far away as India and Britain.

The Minoan language (a non-Greek tongue) became familiar on Thera, and some Therans adopted Minoan dress and, perhaps, other customs. This process speeded up considerably after an even larger earthquake shook the southern Aegean about 1700 B.C. As before, the Therans dutifully rebuilt their damaged homes. On Crete, meanwhile, the Minoans rebuilt their own damaged palace centers, making them larger and more splendid than ever. The one at Knossos became a marvel to behold, covering many acres and, in some places, rising to a height of five stories. In this period, the Minoans also rapidly created an empire, spreading their influence, perhaps, sometimes by force, to many neighboring islands and even to portions of the Greek mainland (where the local residents were still culturally and materially backward).

Awesome Forces Unleashed

This golden age of Minoan cultural and economic splendor was relatively short-lived, however. No one in the region could have imagined the awesome primeval forces that were building beneath their feet and straining to be unleashed. The earthquakes they had experienced in the past were only a small foretaste of the destruction to come. These quakes were part of a grand sequence of geologic events leading up to the biggest outburst of the Theran volcano in more than a million years.

The first of two or more small, preliminary eruptions began sometime between the late seventeenth and late sixteenth century B.C. (Scholars differ somewhat on the exact date.) After an earthquake and an outpouring of ash from one of the volcanic cones, many of Thera's inhabitants left the island. But a brief period of quiet followed, and an unknown number returned and began to go through the ritual of making repairs. Eventually, however, the eruption resumed and worsened. The quaking earth and rains of ash and stones became frightening enough to scare most of the residents away, this time, for good.

Soon, as the eruption approached its terrifying climax, enormous amounts of ash were ejected high into the atmosphere. The ash blocked incoming sunlight and an eerie pall of darkness descended over a huge expanse of the eastern Mediterranean, reaching as far as northern Egypt, more than four hundred miles to the southeast. Giant bolts of lightning temporarily lit up Thera's now blasted and barren landscape, and a series of enormous blasts from the volcanic cones could be heard as far away as India, Britain, Scandinavia, and central Africa.

In an amazingly short span of time, the volcano had belched out more than seven cubic miles of debris. This emptied the immense magma chamber below. For a few, suspenseful minutes, or, perhaps, hours, the massive bulk of the island's central section hung precariously over the frightening void. Finally, it gave way. The collapse of the volcanic cones created a stupendous roar that could be heard over a quarter of the planet's surface. Simultaneously, an airborne shock wave like (that of a nuclear blast) rippled out in all directions and, minutes later, struck the northern coast of Crete with hurricane force.

Meanwhile, the sea rushed into the newly formed caldera, creating huge steam explosions as it came into contact with the hot materials below. At the same time, the sudden displacement of so much water generated a fantastic surge of energy, which now sped outward through the sea at hundreds of miles per hour. In the open Aegean, the tsunamis were barely perceptible as they passed swiftly and silently beneath ships. But as the waves entered the shallows near Crete's northern coast, they reared up into towering walls of water, crashing down and rushing inland, destroying coastal towns and inflicting severe damage on some of the Minoan palace centers. All over the Aegean, huge waves battered the coasts, flattening buildings and crushing or drowning untold thousands. In a cruel twist of fate, quite likely among the dead were the Therans who had recently fled the disaster in their small sailing ships. "Wherever they made landfall, it seems all trace of them has vanished," Rodney Castleden points out:

> It would be pleasant to think of [them] founding a civilized colony somewhere . . . and that one day we will find archaeological evidence of it, but it is more likely that they perished. They would have landed on some Thera-facing shore, drawing their ships onto the beaches, imagining themselves safe,

A Shadow on the Earth

In this excerpt from his book *Unearthing Atlantis*, scientist Charles Pellegrino provides a rather poetic description of the Thera eruption as seen from the surface of the moon.

Down there on earth, the course of history was shifting, shifting like sand from infinite possibilities to the shadow of a dream.

Even from a vantage point on the lunar highlands, you could have seen it without the aid of telescopes or binoculars. A black spot had appeared on the Aegean Sea, perfectly round, vast and cloudlike. It swelled on the planet below, burst up through the atmosphere and started to rain fire down upon Melos, Naxos and Crete. At its center, the island of Thera was not. Walls of water hovered around a hole more than a mile deep. The air was hotter than live steam, hotter than molten lead, hotter than iron emerging white from a furnace. The shadow on the earth grew with extraordinary speed, slashing down ships as it sluiced into the Mediterranean. White clouds formed and vanished on its edges. In less than one hour it widened to two hundred miles, and then to four hundred miles. It rolled over Turkey and Egypt, turned day into starless night, shed some of its heat and ash and velocity, then stumbled eastward. The stain thinned over Syria and Iran, pulled itself apart into long streamers, thinned still more and spread across Asia like ink poured into a saucer of water— except that this ink stain was laced with sheets of brilliant blue lightning.

watching the eruption column growing over their one-time home. They would have unloaded their belongings, making themselves as comfortable as possible in makeshift shelters. Then the tsunamis came to claim them.[57]

The Immediate Aftermath

As the great eruption finally subsided, Thera must have looked nearly unrecognizable to those who had the nerve to sail their vessels near the island. An enormous bay occupied the area where once a range of low mountains had stood. High cliffs, too steep to climb, lined the bay, and the town at Akrotiri had been erased from view, entombed in thick layers of ash and other debris. These investigators likely figured that the gods had damned this place and that

Thera's Waves and the Exodus

Some historians and scientists have suggested that one manifestation of the Thera eruption is recorded in the biblical story of the Exodus, in which Moses parts the Red Sea and the Egyptian army is destroyed in the returning waters. The scholarly jury is still out on this intriguing piece of speculation, summarized here by A.G. Galanopoulos in *Atlantis: The Truth Behind the Legend.*

Biblical scholars have now for many years supported the view that the Israelites crossed, not the Red Sea, but the Sea of Reeds . . . a lake or lagoon [in northern Egypt] . . . separated from the Mediterranean by a narrow sandy strip. . . . The destruction of the Egyptian army could easily be one of the consequences of the tsunami generated by the collapse of the central part of Santorini [Thera], in the following manner. [As the great waves neared Egypt's shores] the water ebbed away. . . . [And] as the sea withdrew, the strip dividing the lagoon from the sea would certainly widen . . . and the lagoon for a while become completely separated from the sea. The Israelites, taking advantage of this opportunity, would then have been able to cross . . . over the new piece of dry land. . . . Normally, tsunamis appear between 15 and 30 minutes after the receding of the sea. In this period of time . . . [the Israelites] would be able to run over the piece of dry land . . . while the sea-wave that swept in after their passage would wipe out the [pursuing] Egyptians.

people should avoid it; indeed, for centuries afterward, Thera remained uninhabited.

Farther south, in Crete, many Minoans had managed to survive the catastrophe. But they had suffered a blow from which they would never completely recover. Many square miles of farmland had been ruined by the ashfall; most buildings near the coasts, where a majority of people lived, had been badly damaged; and most of the merchant vessels and warships had been lifted up by the waves, carried inland, and smashed to pieces. Rebuilding began and, in some places, recovery was significant. But it was a slow, painful process.

Had the Minoans had no enemies or rivals, they might have rebounded fully and gone on to become major players in European history. But they did have enemies—the mainland Mycenaeans. Over the course of the ensuing century, piece by piece, in one military expedition after another, the invaders seized control of Crete. The turnover from Minoan to Mycenaean rule was known to the Egyptians, who had long enjoyed trade relations with Crete. A series of wall paintings found in the tombs of high Egyptian officials, beginning with one dated about 1490 B.C., show Keftiu (Cretans) bearing trade goods. In the first two paintings, the Keftiu wear Minoan-style cutaway kilts. In the third painting, however, their clothes have been painted over to depict wraparound kilts, the style worn by the mainland Mycenaeans. According to J.V. Luce: "The change in this tomb decoration can hardly be discounted as a mere artistic whim. It must surely have political significance. As such, it seems very good evidence for dynastic change at Knossos."[58]

Meanwhile, the Egyptians had noted more than just the regime change in faraway Crete. In the first few years

A photo of the renowned Lion Gate at Mycenae in southern Crete. Mycenaean forces eventually took over Minoan Crete.

following catastrophe, traders from southern Asia Minor and other areas north of Egypt told stories about a terrible disaster. An entire island had sunk into the sea in a single day, they said. At the same time, the Egyptian priests heard disjointed accounts of the sufferings of the Keftiu, who, for a while, stopped visiting the land of the Nile. Minoan merchants eventually reappeared in Egypt, but far less often than before, and in time they stopped coming altogether. In the course of the next few generations, Castleden speculates, the Egyptian priests "compressed and combined the separate though related events: the sudden disappearance of Thera and the more gradual disappearance of the Minoan trading empire."[59] Meanwhile, Mycenaean traders who visited Egypt in these years, including some from Athens, boasted about how their people had, in the recent past, defeated a powerful maritime empire in the great sea west of Egypt.

Memories Lost, Knowledge Regained

More than two centuries passed before a series of invasions, migrations, and other such upheavals rocked the eastern Mediterranean region. The Mycenaean kingdoms collapsed, their fortresses fell into ruin, and a dark age engulfed Greece. In this period, writing disappeared and the transmission of information, including stories about the past, became solely oral. Not until the eighth century B.C., about four hundred years later, did prosperity begin to return and writing reappear (using an alphabet borrowed from a Palestinian trading people, the Phoenicians). By this time, memories of the Bronze Age kingdoms, rulers, and events had become garbled, inflated, and distorted into myths. Homer now recorded a number of these in his great epic poems, the *Iliad* and the *Odyssey*.

Another two centuries elapsed. While visiting Egypt, the Athenian lawgiver Solon confered with priests in the city of Saïs, who told him an intriguing story. First, they made it clear that they knew this extremely antique tale because their civilization was older and wiser than his. "O Solon," one old priest said in Plato's *Timaeus*,

> you Greeks are never anything but children, and there is not an old man among you. . . . There is no old opinion handed down among you by ancient tradition, nor any science which is hoary with age. . . . Whatever happened either in your country or in ours, or in any other region of which we are informed . . . they have all been written down by us of old, and are preserved in our temples. . . . You do not know that there formerly dwelt in your land the fairest and noblest race of men which ever lived, and that you and your whole city are descended from a small seed or remnant of them which survived. And this was unknown to you, because, for many generations, the survivors of that destruction died, leaving no written word.

Then the priests told Solon about the heroic deeds of his ancestors:

> There was a time, Solon, before the great deluge [flood] . . . when the city which now is Athens was first in war. . . . Many great and wonderful deeds are recorded of your state in our histories. But one of them exceeds all the rest in greatness and valor. For these histories tell of a mighty power which unprovoked made an

The ancient Greek statesman Solon brought the tale of Atlantis to Greece from Egypt in the sixth century B.C.

expedition against the whole of Europe and Asia, and to which your city put an end. This power came forth out of the Atlantic Ocean. . . . Now in this island of Atlantis there was a great and wonderful empire which had rule over the whole island and several others, and over parts of the continent.[60]

Solon passed on this story of Atlantis to a relative, who did the same, until it reached Plato almost two hundred years later.

A Place That Should Have Existed

There is no way to know whether Plato believed the story. He might have viewed it as mere mythical fabrication; or he might have felt it had some basis in fact. His view of the truth of the account aside, he definitely recognized it as promising material on which to base a philosophical discussion. The fact that the unfinished *Critias* ends with the gods about to pass judgment on and punish the Atlanteans is revealing of Plato's purpose. It seems almost certain he wanted to make some kind of moral statement about the consequences of a nation becoming corrupt and falling from divine grace. Another theme of his version of the story is the moral superiority of the early Athenians, who remained uncorrupted and bravely faced and defeated a stronger, ruthless aggressor. As scholar Geoffrey Ashe puts it, Plato needed an "edifying contrast and crisis" and found it in

> a massive assault by a huge alien empire, thwarted by the moral fiber of Athens. He wanted such an empire, with freedom to fictionalize. Having resolved to center it on a realm such as Greek images of antiquity (Cretan and otherwise) could suggest—a realm wrecked as a divine judgment by a convulsion of nature—he was able to give that

realm the size he required by locating it in the spacious, uncharted west.[61]

Thus, in reality, it seems that there never was a continent, island, or empire called Atlantis. There was only a legend, based on a hazy, distorted memory of places and events in Bronze Age Greece and passed down through many generations. Yet, until the dawn of the twentieth century, no one realized this was the case. And, so, in the more than two thousand years since Plato penned his account, Atlantis grew into the kind of larger-than-life concept that excites the human imagination. It became an enduring mystery, the fountainhead of civilization, and a symbol of the better world that many yearn for. "Atlantis is not merely a territory swallowed up by the sea," says Ashe:

> It is not merely a theme for geographic debate, or volcanic or seismic speculation. Its spell is inherent, compelling, and strong enough to lend credibility to theories that are often incredible. . . . It stands for the Golden Age and it stands for Ancient

Plato and Political Fable

In his book about Atlantis, scholar Geoffrey Ashe speculates about Plato's literary and philosophical motives in adopting and embellishing the Atlantis story.

Plato was, primarily, creating a myth. That can be said without prejudice to any inquiry into his sources or the factual background. He believed that small well-organized states were better than empires. Empires decayed, city-republics such as Athens had superior moral force, and, though they also could decay, they had a power of regeneration. Not long before Plato's own time Athens had played the leading role in repulsing the aggressive empire of Persia. He evoked an ancient Athens more or less fulfilling his own ideals and thus capable of defeating an even greater empire, the greatest ever. In the making of this political fable, his literary skill—on the face of it—ran away with him, so that he devised a tale far richer, far more circumstantial, than his purpose required.

Wisdom. . . . The Atlantis of modern imagination reflects a desire to draw threads together, to unravel mysteries, to fill what is felt to be a historical gap with . . . a great wonderful Something Else that *should* have existed, and corresponds to perennial [human] yearnings.[62]

Notes

Introduction: Longing for a Land of Beauty and Plenty

1. Jules Verne, *Twenty Thousand Leagues Under the Sea*, trans. Philip S. Allen. 1870. Reprint, Pleasantville, NY: Reader's Digest, 1990, p. 246.
2. Richard Ellis, *Imagining Atlantis*. New York: Random House, 1998, p. 5.
3. L. Sprague de Camp, *Lost Continents: The Atlantis Theme in History, Science, and Literature.* New York: Dover, 1970, pp. 1–2.
4. Camp, *Lost Continents*, p. 277.

Chapter One: Plato's Original Account of Atlantis

5. Plato, *Timaeus*, in *The Dialogues of Plato*, trans. Benjamin Jowett. Chicago: Encyclopaedia Britannica, 1952, p. 444.
6. Plato, *Timaeus*, pp. 445–46.
7. Plato, *Timaeus*, p. 446.
8. Plato, *Timaeus*, p. 446.
9. Plato, *Timaeus*, p. 446.
10. Plato, *Critias*, in *The Dialogues of Plato*, p. 482.
11. Plato, *Critias*, p. 483.
12. Plato, *Critias*, pp. 483–84.
13. Plato, *Critias*, p. 484.
14. Plato, *Critias*, p. 485.
15. Plato, *Critias*, p. 484.
16. Ellis, *Imagining Atlantis*, p. 16.

Chapter Two: The Modern World Rediscovers Atlantis

17. Plutarch, *Life of Solon*, in *The Rise and Fall of Athens: Nine Greek Lives by Plutarch*, trans. Ian Scott-Kilvert. New York: Penguin, 1960, p. 444.
18. Plutarch, *Life of Solon*, p. 76.
19. Proclus, *The Commentaries of Proclus on the* Timaeus *of Plato*, trans. Thomas Taylor. 2 vols. London: privately printed, 1820, vol. 1, pp. 148–49.
20. Camp, *Lost Continents*, pp. 19–20.
21. Ignatius Donnelly, *Atlantis: The Antediluvian World.* 1882. Reprint, London: Sidgwick and Jackson, 1970, p. 479.
22. Donnelly, *Atlantis*, p. 2.
23. Donnelly, *Atlantis*, p. 2.
24. Rodney Castleden, *Atlantis Destroyed.* New York: Routledge, 1998, p. 185.
25. Camp, *Lost Continents*, pp. 42–43.

Chapter Three: Searching for Atlantis Around the Globe

26. Shirley Andrews, *Atlantis: Insights from a Lost Civilization.* St. Paul: Llewellyn, 2001, p. 24.
27. Rachel L. Carson, *The Sea Around Us.* New York: Oxford University Press, 1951, pp. 71–72.
28. Camp, *Lost Continents*, p. 183.
29. Carson, *The Sea Around Us*, p. 72.
30. Carson, *The Sea Around Us*, pp. 72–73.

31. Charles Berlitz, *Atlantis: The Eighth Continent*. New York: G.P. Putnam's Sons, 1984, p. 108.
32. Andrews, *Atlantis*, pp. 241–42.
33. Ellis, *Imagining Atlantis*, p. 77.

Chapter Four: The Atlantean Empire and Minoan Crete

34. Plutarch, *Life of Theseus*, in *Rise and Fall of Athens*, pp. 25–26.
35. K.T. Frost, "The Lost Continent," *Times* (London), February 9, 1909, n.p.
36. Plato, *Timaeus*, p. 446.
37. Frost, "The Lost Continent."
38. Plato, *Timaeus*, p. 441.
39. Castleden, *Atlantis Destroyed*, p. 6.
40. Plato, *Critias*, pp. 483–84.
41. For more detailed discussions of the derivation of the name Atlantis, see Castleden, *Atlantis Destroyed*, p. 168; Camp, *Lost Continents*, pp. 225–26, and especially J.V. Luce, *Lost Atlantis: New Light on an Old Legend*. New York: McGraw-Hill, 1969, p. 180, and Charles Pellegrino, *Unearthing Atlantis: An Archaeological Odyssey*. New York: Random House, 1991, pp. 45–47.
42. Plato, *Critias*, p. 483.
43. Castleden, *Atlantis Destroyed*, pp. 138–39.
44. Luce, *Lost Atlantis*, p. 183.
45. Plato, *Critias*, p. 484.
46. Plato, *Critias*, p. 484.
47. Frost, "The Lost Continent."
48. The possibility remains that Plato based his account on the same oral tradition that inspired Homer and simply fabricated the story about Solon hearing about Atlantis in Egypt. However, if that tradition was still widely known in Plato's own time, it is difficult to understand why other Greek writers did not record or even mention it. It is more likely that the Egyptians preserved the same tradition the early Greeks did and that it died out in Greece before Plato's time.

Chapter Five: Thera and the Blast That Shook History

49. Spyridon Marinatos, "The Volcanic Destruction of Minoan Crete," *Antiquity*, vol. 13, 1939, pp. 429–30.
50. Plato, *Critias*, p. 481.
51. Marinatos, "The Volcanic Destruction of Minoan Crete," p. 426.
52. Luce, *Lost Atlantis*, pp. 83–84.
53. Spyridon Marinatos, "On the Atlantis Legend," *Cretica Chronica*, vol. 4, 1950, p. 210.
54. Hesiod, *Theogony*, in *Hesiod and Theognis*, trans. Dorothea Wender. New York: Penguin, 1973, pp. 50–51.
55. Euripides, *Hippolytus*, in *Three Great Plays of Euripides*, trans. Rex Warner. New York: New American Library, 1958, p. 117.
56. Quoted in Castleden, *Atlantis Destroyed*, pp. 125–26.

Chapter Six: Myths as Memories: The Making of a Legend

57. Castleden, *Atlantis Destroyed*, p. 129.
58. Luce, *Lost Atlantis*, p. 143.
59. Castleden, *Atlantis Destroyed*, p. 175.
60. Plato, *Timaeus*, pp. 445–46.
61. Geoffrey Ashe, *Atlantis: Lost Lands, Ancient Wisdom*. London: Thames and Hudson, 1992, p. 23.
62. Ashe, *Atlantis*, pp. 29–31.

For Further Reading

Books

Giovanni Caselli, *In Search of Knossos: Quest for the Minotaur's Labyrinth.* New York: Peter Bedrick, 1999. Filled with stunning color photos, this excellent book tells about the discovery and excavation of the leading Minoan palace on Crete, the memory of which originally served as part of Plato's inspiration for his Atlantis myth.

Andrew Donkin, *Atlantis, the Lost City.* London: Dorling Kindersley, 2000. A beautifully illustrated discussion of the major theories for the location of Atlantis. Aimed at basic readers.

Don Nardo, *Ancient Philosophers.* San Diego: Lucent, 1994. Contains a useful biography of Plato, whose dialogues introduced the original story of Atlantis.

———, *Krakatoa.* San Diego: Lucent, 1990. This overview of the eruption of the Krakatoa volcano, near Java, in 1883 is useful for its detailed descriptions of a volcanic caldera formation witnessed and documented in modern times. The eruption of the Thera volcano in the Bronze Age, which became part of the Atlantis legend, was similar, but on a much larger scale.

Holly Wallace, *The Mystery of Atlantis.* Chrystal Lake, IL: Heineman Library, 1999. Begins with Plato's dialogues and other early accounts of Atlantis, then explores a number of the locations for the so-called lost continent that have been proposed over the centuries.

Websites

Akrotiri—Lost Atlantis? Peter Lok (www.dragonridge.com). A brief overview of the ancient town of Akrotiri, on the island of Thera, and its connections with the Bronze Age eruption of the island's volcano and possible link to the Atlantis legend. Has some striking photos of the town and surrounding area.

Knossos, Hellenic Ministry of Culture (www.culture.gr). Sponsored by the Greek government, this colorful site provides a useful thumbnail sketch of the great palace that was once the central focus of the Bronze Age Minoan empire. The photos enlarge when clicked.

Where Was Atlantis?, T.J. Elias (www.tje.net). Presents a nice overview of some of the more popular proposals for Atlantis's location, then takes the position that the legend of Atlantis was a distorted recollection of the Minoan civilization on Crete and Thera.

Works by Plato, Internet Classics Archive (http://classics.mit.edu). Provides links to complete English translations of Plato's dialogues (by noted scholar Benjamin Jowett), including the two dealing with Atlantis, the *Timaeus* and the *Critias*.

Major Works Consulted

Geoffrey Ashe, *Atlantis: Lost Lands, Ancient Wisdom*. London: Thames and Hudson, 1992. A brief but brisk and informative synopsis of the history of literature about Atlantis. Also contains several handsome illustrations.

L. Sprague de Camp, *Lost Continents: The Atlantis Theme in History, Science, and Literature*. New York: Dover, 1970. One of the best modern books about Atlantis explores the history of and research into the legend in considerable detail and ends with Camp's conclusion that Atlantis was a literary invention of Plato.

Rodney Castleden, *Atlantis Destroyed*. New York: Routledge, 1998. An information-packed presentation of the now widely accepted theory that the legend of Atlantis was a garbled memory of the Minoan civilization on the islands of Crete and Thera. Highly recommended.

———, *Minoans: Life in Bronze Age Crete*. New York: Routledge, 1993. One of the best available general overviews of Minoan civilization.

Edgar E. Cayce, *Edgar Cayce on Atlantis*. Ed. Hugh L. Cayce. New York: Castle, 1968. A collection of the renowned psychic's "readings" about the lost continent of Atlantis, including his claim that the Atlanteans possessed technology as or more advanced than today's.

Andrew Collins, *Gateway to Atlantis: The Search for the Source of a Lost Civilization*. New York: Carroll and Graf, 2000. Collins, who advocates the idea that Atlantis was in the Caribbean, provides an enormous amount of well-researched information about competing Atlantis theories. Interesting reading.

Ignatius Donnelly, *Atlantis: The Antediluvian World*. 1882. Reprint, London: Sidgwick and Jackson, 1970. The seminal modern work about Atlantis and the gospel of Atlantology, this large book contains a great deal of circumstantial evidence for the existence of an island empire in the Atlantic Ocean in ancient times. Most of Donnelly's claims do not stand up to close scrutiny, but the work is important for the scope of its influence on other researchers and writers.

Richard Ellis, *Imagining Atlantis*. New York: Random House, 1998. A well-written, carefully researched recent study of Atlantis, including a comprehensive overview of the many theories for the lost continent's location. Highly recommended for its fine scholarship and critical judgment.

A.G. Galanopoulos and Edward Bacon, *Atlantis: The Truth Behind the Legend.* New York: Bobbs-Merrill, 1969. This well-written book provides a valuable summary of the early research about the Minoan-Theran connection to the Atlantis legend. Though now somewhat dated, it contains some useful information not discussed in many other books on the subject.

D.A. Hardy, ed., *Thera and the Aegean World III.* 3 vols. London: Thera Foundation, 1990. A collection of essays by noted experts, overall this is a large, fairly up-to-date, and valuable overview of what scholars know about the Minoans and the Bronze Age eruption of Thera, which many scientists and histories think are tied to the Atlantis legend.

J.V. Luce, *Lost Atlantis: New Light on an Old Legend.* New York: McGraw-Hill, 1969. A noted classical scholar weighs in on the Minoan-Theran-Atlantean theory. Luce includes large excerpts from Plato's *Timaeus* and *Critias* and suggests how they might be interpreted in light of archaeological discoveries in Crete and other Aegean sites. Highly recommended.

Spyridon Marinatos, *Excavations at Thera, 1968–1974.* Athens: Athens Museum, 1975. This summary of Marinatos's excavations at the Theran site of Akrotiri is fascinating reading for anyone interested in ancient history and provides important information about the civilization on Thera, as well as the disaster that brought about the island's demise.

James W. Mavor Jr., *Voyage to Atlantis.* 1969. Reprint, New York: Park Street Press, 1996. A fast-paced, informative chronicle of Mavor's adventures with fellow researchers J.V. Luce and Spyridon Marinatos on Thera in the 1960s. Mavor draws a fascinating portrait of behind-the-scenes logistics and politics on an archaeological dig while providing many insights about the possible location of Atlantis.

Charles Pellegrino, *Unearthing Atlantis: An Archaeological Odyssey.* New York: Random House, 1991. A well-written synopsis of the popular theory that the eruption of the Theran volcano in the Bronze Age inspired the legend of the sinking of Atlantis.

Plato, *Critias* and *Timaeus*, in *The Dialogues of Plato.* Trans. Benjamin Jowett. Chicago: Encyclopaedia Britannica, 1952. These two dialogues by Plato contain the original account of Atlantis, making them among the most often quoted of his works. Indispensable to any study of Atlantis.

Plutarch, *Life of Solon* and *Life of Theseus*, in *The Rise and Fall of Athens: Nine Greek Lives by Plutarch*. Trans. Ian Scott-Kilvert. New York: Penguin, 1960. In these excerpts from his famous *Parallel Lives*, Plutarch provides important background information about Plato's ancestor Solon, who heard the story of Atlantis from some Egyptian priests, and summarizes the deeds of Theseus, one of Greece's greatest mythical heroes.

Eberhard Zangger, *The Flood from Heaven: Deciphering the Atlantis Legend.* New York: William Morrow, 1992. A scholarly, insightful study of the Atlantis legend, the book makes an interesting case that the Atlantis legend is a distorted memory of the Trojan War. Zangger's comparison of Plato's Atlantis to an island in Homer's *Odyssey* is compelling and may point to the existence of a lost ancient account on which both may have been based. Young people will find this difficult reading, but history and Atlantis buffs will be fascinated.

Additional Works Consulted

Books

Shirley Andrews, *Atlantis: Insights from a Lost Civilization*. St. Paul: Llewellyn, 2001.

H.S. Bellamy, *The Atlantis Myth*. London: Faber and Faber, 1948.

Charles Berlitz, *Atlantis: The Eighth Continent*. New York: G.P. Putnam's Sons, 1984.

Carl Blegen et al., *Troy: Excavations Conducted by the University of Cincinnati*. 4 vols. Princeton, NJ: Princeton University Press, 1950–1958.

Rhys Carpenter, *Discontinuity in Greek Civilization*. New York: Cambridge University Press, 1966.

Rachel L. Carson, *The Sea Around Us*. New York: Oxford University Press, 1951.

John Chadwick, *The Mycenaean World*. New York: Cambridge University Press, 1976.

V.G. Childe, *The Dawn of European Civilization*. London: Routledge and Kegan Paul, 1957.

Oliver Dickinson, *The Aegean Bronze Age*. New York: Cambridge University Press, 1994.

Christos Doumas, *Thera: Pompeii of the Ancient Aegean*. London: Thames and Hudson, 1983.

Robert Drews, *The Coming of the Greeks: Indo-European Conquests in the Aegean and the Near East*. Princeton, NJ: Princeton University Press, 1988.

———, *The End of the Bronze Age: Changes in Warfare and the Catastrophe ca. 1200 B.C.* Princeton, NJ: Princeton University Press, 1993.

Euripides, *Hippolytus*, in *Three Great Plays of Euripides*. Trans. Rex Warner. New York: New American Library, 1958.

Arthur Evans, *The Palace of Minos at Knossos*. 4 vols. London: Macmillan, 1921–1936.

J. Lesley Fitton, *Discovery of the Greek Bronze Age*. London: British Museum Press, 1995.

Rand Flem-Ath and Rose Flem-Ath, *When the Sky Fell: The Search of Atlantis*. New York: St. Martin's, 1995.

Charles Hapgood, *Maps of the Ancient Sea Kings*. London: Turnstone, 1979.

Hesiod, *Theogony*, in *Hesiod and Theognis*. Trans. Dorothea Wender. New York: Penguin, 1973.

Murry Hope, *Atlantis: Myth or Reality?* New York: Penguin, 1991.

J.V. Luce, *The End of Atlantis.* London: Book Club Associates, 1973.

Nanno Marinatos, *Art and Religion in Thera: Reconstructing a Bronze Age City.* Athens: D. and I. Mathioulakis, 1984.

Anna Michalidou, *Knossos: A Complete Guide to the Palace of Minos.* Athens: Ekdotike Athenon, 1993.

Otto Muck, *The Secret of Atlantis.* London: Collins, 1978.

Pliny the Elder, *Natural History.* Trans. H. Rackham. 10 vols. Cambridge, MA: Harvard University Press, 1967.

Plutarch, *Moralia.* Trans. Harold Cherniss et al. 15 vols. Cambridge, MA: Harvard University Press, 1957.

Proclus, *The Commentaries of Proclus on the Timaeus of Plato.* Trans. Thomas Taylor. 2 vols. London: privately printed, 1820.

Jergen Spanuth, *Atlantis of the North.* London: Sidgwick and Jackson, 1979.

Lewis Spence, *The History of Atlantis.* New York: Bell, 1968.

Chester G. Starr, *The Origins of Greek Civilization: 1100–650 B.C.* London: Jonathan Cape, 1962.

Brad Steiger, *Atlantis Rising.* New York: Berkely, 1981.

A.E. Taylor, *A Commentary on Plato's*

Timaeus. Oxford: Oxford University Press, 1928.

William Taylour, *The Mycenaeans.* London: Thames and Hudson, 1983.

Emily Vermeule, *Greece in the Bronze Age.* Rev. ed. Chicago: University of Chicago Press, 1972.

Jules Verne, *Twenty Thousand Leagues Under the Sea.* Trans. Philip S. Allen. 1870. Reprint, Pleasantville, NY: Reader's Digest, 1990.

Michael Wood, *In Search of the Trojan War.* New York: New American Library, 1985.

Periodicals

Christos Doumas, "The Minoan Eruption of the Santorini Volcano," *Antiquity*, vol. 48, 1982.

T.H. Druitt and V. Francaviglia, "Caldera Formation on Santorini and the Physiography of the Islands in the Late Bronze Age," *Bulletin of Volcanology*, vol. 54, 1992.

K.T. Frost, "The Lost Continent," *Times* (London), February 9, 1909.

———, "The Critias and Minoan Crete," *Journal of Hellenic Studies*, vol. 33, 1913.

Christopher Gill, "Genre of the Atlantis Story," *Classical Philology*, vol. 72, 1977.

C.U. Hammer et al., "Dating the Santorini Eruption," *Nature*, vol. 332, 1988.

Thomas W. Jacobson, "17,000 Years of Greek Prehistory," *Scientific American*, vol. 234, 1976.

John Lear, "The Volcano That Shaped the Western World," *Saturday Review*, November 5, 1966.

Stuart Manning, "The Bronze Age Eruption of Thera: Absolute Dating, Aegean Chronology, and Mediterranean Cultural Interrelations," *Journal of Mediterranean Archaeology*, vol. 1, 1988.

Spyridon Marinatos, "On the Atlantis Legend," *Cretica Chronica*, vol. 4, 1950.

————, "The Volcanic Destruction of Minoan Crete," *Antiquity*, vol. 13, 1939.

J.W. Mavor Jr., "A Mighty Bronze Age Volcanic Eruption," *Oceanus*, April 1966.

D.M. Pyle, "The Global Impact of the Minoan Eruption of Santorini, Greece," *Environmental Geology*, vol. 30, 1997.

Thomas G. Rosenmeyer, "Plato's Atlantis Myth: Timaeus or Critias?" *Phoenix*, vol. 10, 1956.

P.M. Warren, "Minoan Crete and Pharaonic Egypt," in E.V. Davies, ed., *Egypt, the Aegean, and the Levant.* London: British Museum Press, 1995.

Index

Academy, 14, 15
Aegean Sea, 86, 87
Africa, 47–49
Ahmose (pharaoh of Egypt), 81
Akrotiri (Greece), 78, 87
Algeria, 48
alphabet, 35, 90
Ammianus Marcellinus, 31
Amnisos (Greece), 69, 72
Andrews, Shirley, 52–54
animals, 21, 23–26, 57, 64–65
Antillia, 39
archaeological discoveries
  at Akrotiri, 78
  fake/mistaken, 40, 41, 47
  at Knossos, 57–58
  by Marinatos, 67–68, 69–70, 72–74, 77, 78, 81
  Minoan domination and, 59
architecture
  extraterrestrial theory and, 53
  at Knossos, 62–64, 77, 84–85, 89

Aristotle, 15, 29
army, of Atlantis, 21–22
artifacts, 40, 41, 65
  see also archaeological discoveries; architecture
Ashe, Geoffrey, 92
Aspronisi (Greece), 71
Athena, 18–19, 76
Athens (Greece), 18, 22, 39, 55–58, 92
Atlantic Ocean, 17, 33–37, 40–41, 44–47, 59
Atlantis, 93–94
  animals and plants in, 21
  appeal of, 10–13
  architecture and, 53, 62–64, 77, 84–85, 89
  army of, 21–22
  Atlantology, 28, 36, 39–41, 52–54
  Bronze Age and, 35, 39, 55–56, 66
  central metropolis of, 18–21
  climate of, 60
  described in *Timaeus*, 14–18, 26, 43
  destruction of, 36, 37, 69
  extraterrestial theory of, 52–54

as fountainhead of civilization, 34–36
geographical descriptions of, 18, 52, 58–60, 71
government of, 20, 22–23, 61, 66
great plain of, 21–22, 59–60, 66
perceived as real place, 29–32
predictions about, 40
religion and, 10, 23–26, 32, 35
war with Athens and, 18, 22, 39, 55–58, 92
  see also location, of Atlantis
Atlantis Destroyed (Castleden), 72
Atlantis: Insights from a Lost Civilization (Andrews), 52–54
Atlantis of the North (Spanuth), 50
Atlantis: The Antediluvian World (Donnelly), 34–37
Atlantis: The Eighth Continent (Berlitz), 52

Picture Credits

Cover Image: © Fortean Picture Library

© AP Wide World Photos, 51

© Art Resource, NY, 80

© James Davis; Eye Ubiquitous/CORBIS, 16

© Fortean Picture Library, 85, 33, 38

© David Hardy/Photo Researchers, Inc., 13

© Hulton/Archive by Getty Images, 75

© Erich Lessing/Art Resource, NY, 10, 25, 57, 89

Library of Congress, 29

© Gail Mooney/CORBIS, 73, 84

© Michael Nicholson/CORBIS, 63

© Nimatallah/Art Resource, NY, 79

© North Wind Picture Archives, 9, 91

© Peter Phillipp; Viennaslide Photoagency/CORBIS, 67

© PhotoDisc, 36, 48

© Picture History, 34

© Reunion des Musees Nationaux/Art Resource, NY, 19

© Hans Georg Roth/CORBIS, 45

© Scala/Art Resource, NY, 64

Steve Zmina, 71

About the Author

Classical historian and award-winning author Don Nardo has written extensively about ancient Greece and Egypt, the ancient lands that originally produced the Atlantis legend. His books include *Egyptian Mythology, The Ancient Greeks, The Greenhaven Encyclopedia of Greek and Roman Mythology*, studies of ancient Greek and Egyptian weapons and warfare, travel guides to ancient Alexandria and Athens, and literary companions to the works of Homer, Sophocles, and Euripides. On several occasions, Mr. Nardo has visited and studied the sites on Thera, Crete, and the Greek mainland related to the Atlantis controversy. He lives with his wife, Christine, in Massachusetts.